PRISONERS IN THE SHED

THE HARROWING TRUE JOURNEY FROM CAPTIVITY TO HOPE

BELLA HOPE SHILOH

Copyright © 2020 by Bella Hope Shiloh. All rights reserved. No part of this publication may be scanned, reproduced, distributed, or transmitted in any form or by any means, including photocopying, recording, or other electronic or mechanical methods, or utilized by any information storage and retrieval system without the prior written permission of the publisher except in the case of brief quotations embodied in reviews and certain other non-commercial uses permitted by copyright law.

All names and identifying features in this book have been changed to protect identities. Although the author and publisher have made every effort to ensure that the information in the book was correct at press time, the author and publisher do not assume and herby disclaim any liability to any party for any loss, damage, or disruption caused by errors or omissions, whether such errors or omissions result from negligence, accident, or any other cause. Neither the author nor the publisher assumes any responsibility or liability whatsoever on behalf of the consumer or reader of this material.

ISBN: 978-1-7345945-1-5

Cover Design by Emmalee Shallenberger, emmaleedesignsart.com

Book Layout Design by: Kyla Steinkraus

Written by Bella Hope Shiloh, bellahopeshiloh.com

Millstone Light Publications

P.O. Box 604

Pleasant Hill, TN 38578

To contact the author, please email: bellahopeshiloh@gmail.com

To contact publisher, please write to: P.O. Box 604, Pleasant Hill, TN 38578

*To Tanya Wellman,
who knew I wasn't crazy,
and who is truly a rock-star in her sphere of influence.
Thank you for changing lives.*

CONTENTS

Praise for Prisoners In The Shed   vii
Introduction   ix

1. Race Against Time   1
2. The Early Secrets   5
3. Preparing The Way For Crazy   11
4. The Bait   23
5. Till Death Do Us Part   29
6. Early Lessons   33
7. Deception   41
8. Let The Games Begin   47
9. Devaluation   55
10. There Are Always Reasons   61
11. The Shed And The Lie   67
12. The Lies We Tell Ourselves   75
13. Today I Will Be Numb   83
14. Hope Of A Sunflower   91
15. The Floods   99
16. Rats In The Morning   107
17. When Your Soul Is Tired   117
18. Dandelions   123
19. Sometimes The Skies Are Silent   127
20. Running Out Of Time   131
21. When The Decision Is Made For You   141
22. When Nowhere Is Safe   149
23. And Then, Some Of Us Hold Our Organs   157
24. Snapping Point   163
25. When It Finally Has A Name   169
26. When The Ember Glows   173
27. Fighting To Be Free   179
28. Hollywood Didn't Lie   185
29. Almost Free   197
30. When Your Safety Net Fails   203
31. Taking My Chances With Hell   209

32. When Your Soul Demands Peace	215
33. A Miracle Called Hope	219
34. In Search of Peace	223
35. Beginning to Rediscover Something I Never Knew	227
Untitled	229
About the Author	231

PRAISE FOR PRISONERS IN THE SHED

"Riveting, heart-wrenching, a powerful example of resiliency... a story of hope." – Kyla Thorne, Trauma Recovery Coach

"Bella's story is an extraordinary account of hope and perseverance in the midst of astounding abuse. Her account gives great insight into how abusers operate and how one can get caught up in abusive relationships." - Naghmeh Abedini Panahi, Executive Director of Tahrir Alnisa Foundation

"Domestic violence cloaked in religious fanaticism is a terrifying fact of modern reality. Prisoners in the Shed reads like a horror story, all the more chilling because it's true." - Sarah McDugal, Author, Speaker, Abuse Recovery Coach, WildernessToWild.com

"A story of resilience and strength inspires and touches the heart as you read it. Shiloh shares with us an account of what is often not heard of, and often silenced by those who allow such horrific abuse to fester. Her story is likely to inspire other survivors and will challenge the status quo of how abuse festers across the world. Bella Hope's bravery and strength shines in a story that is sure to inspire change." - Ruben Muriente, Outreach Coordinator, Interim Executive Director, Chattanooga Family Justice Center

INTRODUCTION

First they take your voice. This is vital so you can't tell others what is going on.
    Then they take your will.
    Then finally your soul.

It's hard to tell a story about things you don't want to remember, things that you don't want to relive. My therapist says those things are in the past and that they can't hurt me now. I understand what she means by this - they do not affect my everyday life like they used to when I was actually living through them. But they do affect my life every day, sometimes in big, but mostly in small or subtle ways. I am overly cautious, non-trusting of people, on higher alert. Was there a life I was supposed to live that was different than this one?

    I flip through the pages of my book. It is filled with photos of our life in the shed. It gives glimpses of the life we led, and

Introduction

some of the details I forget about until I see the pictures. Then it all comes rushing back.

I can feel the icy cold water of the creek. I can smell the mold, and the smoke from the wood stove. That mix created a very distinct odor, and even now - years later - it makes my stomach lurch. I can see the torn-up insulation that the rats have shredded to make nests for their babies. I can feel the heavy mud boots that were three sizes too big, pushing against my legs, and the gritty dirt that covered the unfinished subfloor beneath my feet. More than anything though, I feel the brokenness and exhaustion of my body.

The memories are still there, etched into my mind. Most of the time I don't want to remember, and thankfully I don't have to. But sometimes my kids will comment on our life then, and I cringe, listening to their memories of their childhood.

"Remember when we lived on the property and had to go to the bathroom in that bucket? I hated it because it stunk so bad. So usually, I would just go hide behind that huge sand pile and pee in the grass…"

I always try to bring the conversation back to a positive note with "Isn't it great we don't live like that anymore?" but, truth be told, it doesn't really make me feel any better. Though it has been years, I still have not recovered entirely.

But now we have a second chance. A chance to live a life in freedom. An opportunity to enjoy the simple pleasures of life without the fear-mongering, walking on eggshells, and the lies and darkness that held us captive for so many years. And of course, free from the shed and the man who caged us in with the deceptive titles of "home" and "husband." We can live with hope.

Hope. It was the one thing that kept me going when I didn't have *anything* else. And I believe it is the key to living a beautiful and amazing life, no matter what catastrophe we find ourselves in. It is what makes us bulletproof, invincible. *Warriors*.

It is not the strongest who survive. It is the ones who have hope. Because you can break the human mind. You can break the human spirit. But those who have hope - you can't break them. Their arsenal is far more powerful than you can ever imagine.

Every good Hollywood movie contains a story of overcoming. People want to believe that love always overcomes hate, good overcomes evil, courage triumphs over fear, and truth eventually prevails over lies. We crave these endings – it is what gives us faith to keep going in our real worlds that exist outside of the theater.

My story is none of that… and all of that. If a paradox ever existed, you will find it in these pages. Rather than a story of faith being built, it is about faith being unraveled…which ultimately leads to real faith being discovered. Instead of a fictional story of a hero slaying dragons, it's a true story of getting lost in the darkness… to ultimately find the light. It's a story of a long-fought bloody battle… that eventually leads to a life of peace and contentment. It's the best and worst story you'll read.

But it wasn't concocted in Hollywood. It's true. I lived it, survived it, and now share it with others to give hope. Welcome to my world.

"It is not the strongest who survive. It is the ones who have hope. Because you can break the human mind. You can break the human spirit. But those who have hope…you can't break them. Their arsenal is far more powerful than you can ever imagine." - Bella Hope Shiloh

1
RACE AGAINST TIME

I race as fast as my four-year-old legs can carry me. The steps feel big, but I scramble fast. I am up both flights of stairs in a seeming instant, yet never quick enough for me. I reach the third story of the townhouse, which consists only of the master bedroom and two closets. It is my least favorite place in the house, but it puts the furthest distance between me and them, and gives me the most time to get away.

I never consider hiding in the closets. One is filled with typical clothes - dresses and skirts worn once a year, shoes, and a heavy wooden trunk. Not much place to hide. The second closet holds his arsenal of weapons, MREs (military meals), gas masks, and bullet-proof vests. I never understood what they were for, but I knew it was a secret, and that door remained locked. Hiding isn't good enough anyway. They know where I am.

I run over to the window and frantically try to raise the metal rail to open it. It is heavy and only lifts a few inches. A frigid breeze flows in, fanning my hope, and I pull harder, forcing the weighty frame up enough for me to potentially squeeze through the opening. I push the screen out. It free falls and disappears. I look down and see the deck, three stories below. I pause for only a split second - *then jump out.*

In some dreams, I am able to fly. I try desperately to swim through the air, struggling hard against the gravity that feels like a lead weight, pulling me down. If it drags me all the way to the ground, I sprint down the sidewalks, my heart thumping in my chest as if it is about to burst. I dart behind bushes, trying to slip unnoticed between houses and fences… fleeing to get away. My lungs feel like they will collapse from the effort.

In other dreams I fall, but in slow motion. Sometimes I land on top of the fence that separates our yard from the neighbors. I bounce - as if my feet have springs - down to the neighbor's deck and scramble away as fast as possible. My goal is to get to other neighborhoods, and hide. The impending doom is overwhelming. They are always right on my trail.

This recurring dream will play over and over throughout the next twenty years, jarring me out of sleep and forcing me to ask the questions: Who are they? And what is going on inside our home that is so bad a child would rather jump out of a three-story building than remain inside?

I always knew the answer to the first question - it was my parents. More specifically my father. They wanted to catch me, to keep me from escaping. But the answer to the second question remains a partial mystery. I know intrinsically it involves sexual abuse from my father. Somewhere in the vast catalog of memories tucked away in different portions of my brain, fragmented thoughts occasionally bubble to the surface of my conscious mind. I have flashes of images that, even while they surface, I try to keep buried, unexposed. Sometimes I am frustrated because the memories remain dark, like a thick fog. Yet the feelings they elicit are like sharp shards of glass, etching pathways through my mind, and more so my body, which has held in a feeling of terror and pain for decades.

Some days I believe if I could only sharpen the image - replay the full memories rather than just their parts, and unlock the unspoken and unremembered events - that somehow it would release me into a realm of healing that now seems absolutely impossible. Will I ever be free?

As a four-year-old, when I am awake and not dreaming, I go to my brother's room on the second story and look out the window. A few feet below is the triangular overhang that shelters the front door of our house. If there was ever a fire or emergency, I think that perhaps I could climb out onto the overhang, then jump down to the grass. It looks far down, but maybe, since I am four, I could bounce? A child's mind does not grasp that gravity is an uncompromising law of nature, and that I would no doubt break many bones in my body, or die. But in the dream, I always jump. It always seems safer.

2

THE EARLY SECRETS

I remember the day I became a statistic. I guess I had already been one for many years, so it's more accurate to say I remember the day I *realized* I was a statistic. It made me angry. *So angry.*

They say that abused children grow into adults who perpetuate the cycle by becoming abusive, or they marry an abuser. I thought I had broken that cycle. I had sworn that generational curse would not affect me or my children. We would do things different; we would *not* follow suit. Or would we?

I was raped before I was old enough to write my own name. My father was big into pornography, and, as reputed, it led him further and further into darkness until it seemed a desirable thing to destroy a four-year-old little girl for the sake of a few seconds of pleasure. Sick pleasure. Demented, twisted pleasure.

An eight-year-old daughter should never be raised to be a

prostitute. Yet my father reinforced his agenda - and my identity - when, while molesting me over the years, he repeatedly told me he was "preparing me for my future."

The next nine years of molestation was a battle - a war against shame that carved up my soul and slaughtered my innocence. It never occurred to me to tell. Something so vile and despicable was understood to be a secret. A child has neither the language nor mental construct to understand incest, and how can she relate what she does not understand?

Even as an adult, there are things too dark to speak about. To describe these crimes only creates images of horror in the hearer that time does not erase. It is enough to say, a man's depravity knows no boundaries.

As children, my siblings and I suffered from physical, mental, emotional, verbal, and sexual abuse. Our parents worked different shifts. It was way too easy for him to get drunk, abuse us, and go back to work before my mother came home. We acted as if everything was normal. It *was* our normal. We didn't know that it wasn't supposed to be that way.

Like kids do, we all compensated in different ways. My brother acted out in violence and obsessive-compulsive behaviors, my sister withdrew into denial, believing it didn't affect her at all. I became a people-pleaser and perfectionist.

I got great grades in school and entered high school when I was only 12 years old. I was known as "the smart kid." I started college at 16, with the goal to become a doctor. I graduated with honors or summa cum laude from every school I attended, and with every certificate I was awarded. I had a photographic memory and could recite entire pages by memory. I was detail oriented. I hyper-focused on what I could control (which wasn't much).

The energy it takes to conceal secrets of that magnitude, however, is exhausting. It drains you of vitality, of life. The only way to survive such trauma is to numb your mind and emotions. You pretend and you deny. You distract. You build walls. Your insides may be shattered but you can't worry about that…you have to keep on doing your daily things. I played the part I was expected to. I was the good girl, the smart girl, the obedient girl. Inside I was the broken girl, the confused girl, the exhausted girl.

I believed the lies: I was not loved. It was my fault. I was worthless, merely an object. The world is completely unsafe and so are people. You can't trust anything or anyone, etc.

For 15 years I kept the secrets. Despite my courageous outward facade, the stress took a toll on me physically. My immune system was compromised, and I had a weak constitution because I internalized everything. At fourteen-years-old I developed stomach ulcers which came and went for the next several years. By nineteen, one of those ulcers almost perforated my stomach. I developed severe vomiting and could not even hold down water. Thankfully, a hospital visit and stomach scope revealed the problem before I required emergency surgery. My body understood what I was mentally denying - I was *not* okay.

My childhood was a confusing combination of "normal" and "bizarre." It was as common to be raped as it was for me to ride my bicycle. Though we roller-skated, played hide-and-seek and baseball, and swam at the pool like all normal kids, we also were exposed to pornographic videos and other lewd materials.

The biggest contributor to this bizarre blend was my father, Warner. It might be rightfully said that he was mentally ill but maybe he was just drunk all the time, I don't know. Either can bring out the crazy in people. His belief system was ever-changing and extreme. As a child I didn't understand how radical his beliefs were. There are vague memories that surface from time to time, and now with an adult's comprehension of the facts, I wonder "What version of crazy *was* that?"

Warner was an ex-military man who despised the government and believed it was plotting mass murder. His goal was to gather an arsenal of weapons and one day form his own militia. I'm unsure who was to compose this militia, but I knew I was expected to be a side-kick. When I was nine years old, he entered my sister and I into the local BB gun club to learn how to shoot. Although I was proud when I hit the target, I was resentful of having to spend my Saturdays in a musty-smelling building full of taxidermies - stuffed deer, elk, and moose heads, and a ghastly buffalo head that hung above the stairs. The people there were rugged, rough, and intimidating, holding staunchly to their semi-unspoken motto of "kill them before they kill you."

Attending gun shows was common for us as kids, and Warner would buy guns and knives and dehydrated MRE's to stockpile. I think he was preparing for "the end times." I remember when I was eight years old he made me try on a bulletproof vest and gas mask he had bought. The mask looked like a massive fly and scared me stiff! He showed me how it worked, and handed me a filter that attached to the snout of the mask, which I thought was a "can of air." He informed me I would have to wear this "when the shit hits the fan."

"What happens when you run out of cans of air?" I asked.

He laughed. "It's all over then!"

With each odd incident, a seed of fear was planted. I knew something cataclysmic was coming, but I didn't know what. I thought for sure one day we would suffocate to death because we would run out of "cans of air," while hiding in the back closet of our townhouse, away from evil men in black suits who would try to raid our house.

My parents bought property in Montana in the mountains.

There was talk about building an underground house, and I vaguely remember seeing professional plans my father had sent away for, from a company that was selling the idea and/or materials. The drawings depicted an underground bunker that looked similar to an alien spacecraft with a tunnel attached to the top of it. I hated dark and claustrophobic places. I secretly prayed to the universe that these plans would fail.

I think this is where my mother put her foot down - she palliated my father's obsession for guns, but she didn't want to live in the dark like a mole either. They finally settled on a log cabin idea in the middle of nowhere instead. I was relieved!

Growing up with strange and secretive ideas propagated by my father, the path was paved for tolerating extreme, abusive behaviors from my future husband, Devlin. While I never adopted Devlin's ideas as normal or desirable, by the time he started forcing them on me, I was already trapped. I never imagined it would end the way it did.

3

PREPARING THE WAY FOR CRAZY

I wasn't born crazy. Maybe some folks are. I am sure there is a debate out there somewhere about whether people are born nuts or if they become that way. A nature versus nurture dispute. Probably both are true.

I had multiple sessions with my trauma counselor about the subject of "crazy," because I felt so crazy in the beginning. That's what brainwashing will do to you.

"This is crazy! I feel crazy!"

"*You* aren't crazy. You've just had a *lot* of crazy *done to* you."

Clarity. I've had crazy done to me.

"Nobody chooses to live this way on purpose!" I wailed back.

She sat silently and listened. I guess she was giving me time to continue, or time to dwell on my own thoughts. I hated when she gave that pause because I didn't know what to do with it.

She finally spoke. "What's so bad about crazy anyway? Everybody's a little crazy."

She would know. Her entire career was to listen to crazy.

Her goal was to provoke me to question everything I had been systematically trained to believe, because that would mean ultimate freedom from the lies and deception that made my life feel like a train wreck. But right then I wasn't interested in long-term goals. I wanted more reassurance and validation. And I wanted *him* to be wrong.

"If there's anybody crazy in this world, it's him, not me!"

She agreed.

One of Devlin's main goals was to convince me I was nuts - that I didn't remember things properly, that the things I experienced were just figments of my imagination. He wanted me to believe the abuse he perpetrated upon us was not that bad, and that I was just "exaggerating" or "blowing things out of proportion." If *I* was "crazy," then it validated *him*.

Oh, heck no!

I knew enough by that point to know he was not okay in the head. I had enough factual knowledge of our situation - and trust in my own guts - to know that his actions were not normal and not right. But the voices were there - the voices in my head. Not audible voices; rather memories of the propaganda of people in the cult, who, in so many words, validated his idea that I must be exaggerating what had happened. The tapes played on a continual loop in my mind.

"God hates divorce."

"God will not protect you or your children if you do something He hates."

"We don't believe you."

At that time I called them my "church" and had high regard for their opinion. But this was too much. It fueled a fury within me. Thank God for that fury. It is what kept me alive.

∾

I first met the cult when I was fifteen. (It is where I also met Devlin. And people think the internet is the worst place to meet a spouse! Ha!) My father was introduced to it through one of his friends, and as a family we attended one of their "church services." They claimed to be a church, but they were not. Their control, brainwashing, and crazy theology was nothing short of cultish thinking and behavior, and, like all cults, it was hard to get out of.

My first impression of that service was, "These people feel dead." The atmosphere was silent, stoic, and... well, lifeless. It felt like everyone was holding their breath and edgy. My father told me that we were just used to "liberalism" in the church we had formerly attended, and I would "get used to" the quiet demeanor of this new place.

Within the next few years I got deeply involved in it. I read their books and literature on "the proper way to interpret the Bible" (so that, of course, it matched up with their various beliefs). I sat through sermons, watched videos, and attended meetings - all which indoctrinated me to believe that they, exclusively, possessed the knowledge of "the truth." To Reformers, the only way to get to heaven was to obey implicitly everything you were taught.

Their church was very strict. Some local organizations were more conservative, others were more liberal with what they called their "standards." The local group I was a member of was one of the strictest anywhere, mainly due to two of the leaders who had a reputation for being extreme in their ideas.

They made rules about what you could and could not eat, both publicly and at home. Meat was forbidden. Dairy, cheese, eggs, sugar, white flour, condiments like ketchup, mustard, pickles, or chocolate were a sign that you were "spiritually declining" and not capable of making wise or practical decisions for your life (therefore also affecting what activities you could or could not participate in in the church).

Coffee and tea were off limits, so was anything containing baking soda. If you intentionally ate foods that were genetically modified, or if you ate anything with any oil in it, you were sinning against God. Eating between meals - even a raisin - was wrong. You had to drink water an hour before eating, and not during. Two meals a day was stressed as "superior" to three meals, and therefore the "holier" people followed a twice-a-day schedule.

Women must wear skirts, never pants. Skirts had to be "longer than nine inches off the floor." The "holier" people wore long-sleeved shirts all year, even in ninety degree weather. The "less holy" ones wore t-shirts in the summer and exposed their bare arms. Short sleeves could never be worn in the church, neither shoes that left your toes "naked" - it was considered irreverent and an insult to God. Jewelry was forbidden, so were tie tacks. If the buttons on your shirt were not plain enough or your hair barrette was "too fancy," comments were made by the leadership that you needed to shape up. I remember an elderly lady confronting my ten-year-old daughter one day at church. She looked at the plain little flower barrette she was wearing and asked in a judgmental huff, "Do you really think Jesus wants you wearing *that*!?"

Hair was another issue. Women had to have their hair at least one inch below their shoulders. There were questions about whether bangs were appropriate or not. Dancing, television, movies, and card playing was forbidden, as were all sports. Holidays and birthdays were not celebrated, but looked down upon.

Even church events like communion - meant to draw people together - became an opportunity to wield power and control. They believed that in order to signify unity, everybody had to go through a ceremony of drinking grape juice out of one single cup. Despite protest against it due to the risk of herpes, mononucleosis, and other communicable diseases, they declared, "God will protect us from that." To illustrate this point, they told stories about sharing the communion cup with people who had disease, yet they didn't catch it because "God wouldn't let that happen." They also claimed the sterling silver cup used for the service contained "antibacterial properties" and would kill any microorganisms that touched the surface anyway. Compliance was mandatory.

Communion crackers were another issue. I was once publicly shamed in front of the entire church for not taking a cracker, despite the fact that I was seriously allergic to them and would be in bed with terrible cramps and pain for a week if I did. "It's the least you can do to show your unity to Christ."

Then there were beliefs that were not bad in and of themselves, but were made into measuring sticks to judge how "spiritual" people were. Country living, for example, was promoted. Sermons were given about the benefits of raising families in the country where they would be surrounded by nature. Personally, I always wanted to live in the country - to have space for my kids to run, animals for them to play with, to be able to grow a little garden, and enjoy the fresh air. I loved the mountains. But over time, an attitude arose that those who did not live in the country didn't want what was best for their families and would be "destroyed in the last days" if they didn't get out of the cities fast enough. It became a message of fear and survival, and in order to be "closer to God and free from the corrupting things of city life," people needed to migrate fast and furiously. When Devlin made a plan to isolate us later, this was a huge contributing factor to my agreeing with him. His end goal was to control us more, but he hid it under the guise of "healthy country living" where we would "be safer, like the church teaches."

In the church, we were also taught to shun family and friends who did not believe the same. They were classified as "irreligious relatives" who didn't understand the great truths that we did, and therefore would contaminate our thinking patterns and influence us to give up what we believed was right. The church was very polarizing. They had an "us versus them" mentality. It was "us against the world" or "us against those who would pull us away from our beliefs." Anyone outside the group was suspicious and not to be fully trusted. Former members of the church were considered especially dangerous - they were "led away by Satan"; deceived souls intent on deceiving others.

Aside from all the lifestyle rules, the belief system was typical in the fact that it was a fundamentalist, male-dominated system that claimed strict authoritarian rule. Women were to submit to their husbands in everything. They were relegated to gender-specific roles such as teaching the children or being in charge of cooking. Women were not to speak from the pulpit to teach men ever, except in very rare cases where men were not available in a newly-established group. There were deeply-ingrained misogynistic attitudes, which even the women promoted. Church authority was considered the voice of God. They used Matthew 16:19 to promote this authority ("I will give unto thee the keys of the kingdom of heaven, and whatsoever thou shalt bind on earth shall be bound in heaven, and whatsoever thou shalt loose on earth shall be loosed in heaven") and to disfellowship - or remove from church membership - anyone who was not following their rules, or anyone who they thought was unworthy.

Private and public shaming was the main way they controlled their members. Everyone watched each other for unacceptable behavior, and tattling to the leaders was seen as virtuous and necessary to keep the church "pure." If they identified something in your life they thought was inappropriate, they would call you into a private "discussion" in a closed room, with five other people who were considered superior. During this time, they told you what your offense was and what you needed to change. The language was heavily laden with words like "duty," "sin," "God's requirements," and "submission." Guilt was driven into your soul with humiliation and social pressure. If you did not repent of your misguided thoughts or deeds, this group would go before the entire church and expose your "sin" to the entire congregation, who would then vote on whether or not to kick you out of "God's church," and if not, what other measures were to be done to you.

Being out of the church, of course, meant you were eternally damned and would go to hell. This was based on their favorite line: "Connection with God involves connection with His church," implying that by not being a member of the church you had severed your connection with God.

Because of this "church," when I married Devlin I had already been well-indoctrinated to submit to other people's control. Other people's minds dictated what my life was supposed to look like. I remember the church leader proclaiming one time in a sermon that, "If you live by our principles - *which are God's principles* - most of the decisions you have to make in life, have already been made for you." It is eerie now when I think about it – that he was admitting, in a way, to brainwashing others, while the brainwashed members sat and listened silently, nodding their heads in agreement.

With only a few exceptions, I complied with everything I was told to do. I was the "good girl," after all. I believed it was my duty and responsibility to be obedient and submissive. Religious quotes were used against me to back up these ideas. Because of this, my opinions and free will were slowly but steadily stripped away from me.

Successful control of another human being does not happen overnight. It is done slowly over time until you are conditioned to obey what you are told without question. You don't even have to be conscious of the process for it to be effective; in fact, it is often subconscious. Complete control almost always involves a process of brainwashing and one of the most disturbing parts is that you don't even know it is happening.

This was true, both of the church, and of Devlin. I was unaware what they were turning me into. My people-pleasing nature made it so easy for them to manipulate me and I was taught to rationalize away all the warning signs. This was done mainly by well-composed *implications*:

- The rules were not called rules - they were called "standards" - *God's* standards to be exact.
  Upholding them was not *arbitrary*, they said; rather, obeying *joyfully* was evidence of *a willing heart*.
  Implication: Who doesn't want to show a willing heart towards God and follow His expectations?
- Those who obeyed the dietary restrictions were not being *legalistic*, they were merely choosing "the best foods to nourish a clear mind" so that God could have full access to impress them with truth.
  Implication: Do you want to have an unclear mind so that God cannot reach you?
- Since God is "a God of order and punctuality," those who showed up late to church for whatever reason were "not making the best use of their God-given time, and delays tire the angels."
  Implication: All heaven and earth is distressed

when you are late for a service, and it must not continue.

- Because God organized His church and made leaders over groups, those who do not submit are in rebellion against God. After all, 1 Samuel 15:23 says "rebellion is as the sin of witchcraft, and stubbornness is as iniquity and idolatry. Because thou hast rejected the word of the LORD, he hath also rejected thee." Implication: Every time you do not submit to church authority you are basically practicing witchcraft and are in danger of being rejected by God and sent to hell.

With this system in place, it was easy for Devlin to manipulate every aspect of my life after we got married. My tender conscience made me an easy target to be controlled by fear and false guilt, though I honestly believed I was "doing right for the sake of pleasing God." Devlin's threats toward me were hardly ever direct - rather they were thinly-veiled threats with implied danger attached to every sentence. I remember a sign once that said, "You can accomplish a lot with a smile. You can accomplish even more with a smile and a loaded gun." This is the most accurate way to describe how he leveled his threats at me. His "gun" was invisible to others, but well understood by me.

Like the church, Devlin had rules about everything. They were more extreme in nature than the Reformer's though. Of course, these rules only applied to me and the kids, not to him, and he always had a "good reason" for each rule he created.

I could not have a cell phone because it would "radiate my brain and cause tumors," yet he was allowed to have one because it was "necessary for his business." His rationalization: He only wanted what was "best" for me.

I could only buy a certain brand of peanut butter that came in a glass jar, because buying peanut butter in plastic jars was not allowed. Rationalization: The plastic might "cause us health problems."

He told me to give away the jars of spaghetti sauce I bought and "make it from scratch instead" because the jars contained 2 teaspoons of sugar which was "unhealthy" (yet, when he bought the same exact spaghetti sauce when he was hungry, it was okay). Again, the rationalization was that he only wanted the "healthiest" for our family.

There was no eating out, ever. We were vegan, and even if a bean burrito on the menu was entirely vegan, it was "still made in the same kitchen as hamburger meat, and therefore may have been cross-contaminated." He also didn't want to use the silverware at a restaurant, as a fork would definitely have been used by "meat-eaters" and "probably wasn't washed properly."

Then there were rules about the weekend. The only activity I ever remember doing as a family was going for a walk on Saturday. Saturday was our "church day" and the only activities that could be done besides attending church services, were coloring, watching a nature video, or going for a walk. Rules for the walk included not being able to pick flowers, not picking up sticks, and if we happened to come across wild blackberries (which grew prolifically in our area) we were not allowed to pick or eat even one, because "eating between meals" was not allowed, and picking anything on Saturday would incur the wrath of God. You could not run - you needed to walk, on the path, in a straight line.

Another rule was that I was the only one allowed to take care of the children. This applied 24/7. Nobody could babysit or watch the kids besides me. For the first 9 years I was not away from them for a single day.

Over time, Devlin became paranoid. His favorite topics of

discussion were the evils of the world and how the government was plotting against us. Also, he harped on the necessity of organic food and staying "uncontaminated" from the world. Eventually these became the only things he would talk about. He was fearful and distrusting of almost everyone, and he despised authority figures. At first, I thought this was because he grew up in Romania during communism. I thought he had some unhealed wounds from childhood and unbalanced perspectives. But it was more than that - much more. His paranoia of being "contaminated" led to new ideas.

He decided that the kids should not be allowed to go into Walmart because it had too much "worldly stuff in it." He particularly hated the televisions and thought that the kids would be ruined if they happened to look in the direction of the flashing screens. Water fountains were evil because the water had chlorine and fluoride, and it was better for them to be dehydrated and thirsty then to consume water that was "not 100 percent pure." The first time my children ever drank from a water fountain was when they were 9, 11, and 13 years old. They didn't even know how to work one.

I remember listening to him tell me his plans for our next vehicle. He wanted to buy a used van and remove the seat furthest in the back. Then he wanted to build a toilet in that space so that we would "never have to visit a public restroom again." Public restrooms were evil because of the occasional vandalism and foul writing some people did on the stalls, and our children were not to be exposed to that.

I roll my eyes now at all the petty, paranoid things he made rules about, but it was how we lived. Or at least how he expected me and the kids to live.

"Nobody chooses to live this way on purpose!"
No, they don't.

4

THE BAIT

Nobody falls in love with a monster. The evil man is not the version you fall in love with in the beginning. Nope, they are charming. Charismatic. They act kind, compassionate. It's the rose that attracts, not the thorns.

Love-bombing. It's such a fitting phrase. It is a combination of two words that describe the most life-giving thing on earth - love - and the most destructive weapon on the planet. "Love-bombing" is the term used to describe the practice of lavishly showering someone with attention, affection, gifts, compliments, etc., for the purpose of future manipulation. It is the first stage in the cycle of abuse and is very different from genuine acts of kindness performed by someone who loves you. People who love-bomb have a goal in mind, and the sweet words and grand gestures they do are only tools to accomplish their mission. They exhibit warmth, tenderness, and caring. They pour on the affection, and become super accommodating to your needs and wants. They call you on the phone "just to hear your voice" because they feel like you are "such a part of them." They show up at your job with roses to let you know how special you are to them.

This concentrated onslaught of attention creates a false sense of closeness. This is strategic, because it gets you hooked into the relationship prematurely, and gives you memories of "the good times" for when the abuse begins later on. These feelings and seemingly "loving" experiences are what motivate you to forgive and reconcile with them after an abusive explosion that would otherwise have you running away.

Love-bombing accurately describes Devlin's actions towards me initially. He was sweet, he was caring. He would bring me little gifts and flowers often, "just because." He would call me on the phone and we would have long conversations about anything and everything. He did the little things, like filling my car up with gas and opening doors for me. He always tried to make me laugh. As time went on, he ramped up the attention. He moved to California to work as a leader for the church there, and since I lived in Virginia we began a long-distance relationship. He made up for it with almost daily phone calls, cards, and emails. He made us feel connected.

Then there were the surprise visits. Sometimes he would just show up at my apartment, without warning, having flown cross-country just to spend time with me for a few days. He started flying to Virginia once a month, or every other month, to visit.

There are two things most prominent in my memory. First, was the time he flew all night, with layovers, from one side of the country to another, just to spend half a day with me. I picked him up from the airport that morning and drove him back in the late afternoon; we literally spent a few hours together at the beach. He told me it was so worth it just to see me.

The second thing was when my car broke down the following year, and he bought me a new one. It was a pre-owned car, but new to me. I couldn't believe it. Not many guys buy their girlfriend a new car, and I had never owned such a nice one! He made me feel special and taken care of - something completely new to me. I took the bait.

It was this intense bonding process that prepared the way for him to begin changing me into what he wanted. He subtly made his preferences known. He told me how much he liked certain foods, and was *so very* appreciative when I would make those dishes during his visits. Some of the gifts he bought me were clothes - sending a hint of what he thought would "look good" on me. When he flew in for a visit, he packed his carry-on bag with produce from his garden and elaborated on how important garden-fresh food was, and how his mom would can hundreds of quart jars full of fruits and vegetables every year (he later expected the same from me). It was a combination of dumping information on me, with subtle hints of ways to make him happy. I made the mental notes; I cared about him.

As our relationship progressed, he started testing my boundaries. This was especially true with affection - he would try to see how far I would let him get physically. The church had strict boundaries about what was acceptable between males and females, and a "chaperone" was pretty much expected at all times. Of course, Devlin didn't follow these rules - he rather tried to be secretive about our time together.

When we attended events hosted by the church, he would keep the proper distance as he was expected to - especially with him being a leader and all. Conservative evangelical Christianity at that time was going through a shift in ideas about dating and "courtship," as they called it, and a trend was birthed that promoted an entirely hands-off physical relationship until after you were married. Holding hands was the only acceptable form of affection - once you were actually engaged, that is. The church adopted this mentality. Though many individuals had differing ideas about what was acceptable and what was not, they tended towards extremism.

I remember one day sitting at a picnic table together with Devlin eating lunch (in the broad daylight) with several other friends. As they finished eating, one by one our friends left the table until it was only Devlin and I left. Later that day I got reprimanded and shamed by two different adults about how "inappropriate" it was for us to eat lunch together. Apparently, talking with each other over salad and garlic bread was akin to sexual immorality. Another time, we were sitting in chairs in the main meeting hall during a conference, chatting during the time between meetings, and again, in plain sight of everyone so there could be no chance of inappropriate conduct or "an appearance of evil." A church member soon came up to us and joined in our conversation for a few minutes. After an awkward pause, he looked at both of us and said that he would need to chaperone our conversation from there on, because certainly it would be inappropriate for us to have conversation "alone." Talking about the pets we had growing up, or sharing funny stories about childhood, was apparently equivalent to word porn. It was these extreme ideas that drove relationships into secrecy in general, and made me agree with Devlin's conclusion that "the less they know the better." We started spending time together away from everyone else. That brought with it, however, no accountability for Devlin, and since he was not the sort of man who could be trusted, things ended up badly. He continued pushing the limits until, right before we were engaged, he sexually violated me when I was taking a nap.

Big. Red. Flag.

Of course my response as a "good Christian" was to

forgive his major "lack of discretion," and remember that the Bible taught "love covers a multitude of sins." I loved him, and thought I should just let it go and move forward, more carefully this time. After all, he was so "repentant." Crocodile tears lined his lower eyelids while he begged me to forgive him, telling me he didn't deserve me, and that he had just gotten carried away because he was so attracted to me. Not to mention, he was a leader, and it would ruin his reputation, and mine.

Big. Fat. Mistake.

Sexually imposing yourself on someone when they are not even conscious is considered assault, is never an accident, and should never be ignored. I didn't know this. Before he ever asked me to marry him, he had figured out to what lengths he could violate my boundaries, and I would just forgive, stay with him, and try to move past it. Now the destructive part of "love-bombing" would occur; the part that would destroy the girl in me who still had a beautiful spark of life. The girl who believed in joy and happiness, despite childhood trauma. The girl who had a passion for life, and a hope for an amazing future. That spark would be annihilated.

5

TILL DEATH DO US PART

If anyone's marriage should have worked out, it should have been ours. At least that's what I believed. After all, we were doing things the "ideal way" as we had been taught. We had met in church, went through a two-year "missionary school" together, and he became a leader over three churches in three different states. We shared the same beliefs and openly discussed the hard issues. We didn't rush things - we knew each other three years before he proposed. Despite his little "transgression" physically, we had followed the rules, so therefore had more of a chance of a successful marriage than other people who "did it wrong" ... didn't we?

We got married in a garden surrounded by periwinkle dresses and yellow gerbera daisies. They helped offset the grey, darkening skies that threatened a downpour. It was as if even the sky knew this wedding was a bad idea, and it gave us warning in a bad omen.

My girlish daydreams had always portrayed my wedding as one of the happiest days of my life. Yet amid the smiles of guests and piano music, I felt off. I was not sure how one was supposed to feel on their wedding. I had heard about bundles of nerves, stress, happiness, excitement, sentimentalism, joyfulness, etc. I felt strangely lonely.

Chalking it up to my eternal feeling of brokenness, I decided the hype of weddings and touted exhilarated feelings must be due more to Hallmark cards and Hollywood advertising than actual reality. After all, the church taught that "Love is a choice, a decision; not a feeling. Feelings change. If you only love when you have loving feelings, that's not love, it's infatuation. Love is a plant. You must water it. Don't trust your feelings, they are too flighty." But I didn't feel loved, even on that day.

The ceremony went off without too much drama, despite the flower girl who became too shy to walk down the aisle. Afterwards, we took pictures around the gazebos and palm trees while guests made their way to the reception hall a few miles away. It didn't rain; I was glad for that. But by the evening, after cake cutting and speeches, I really wanted to leave. I felt like a stick-in-the-mud for not reveling in the festivities, but I was tired and still feeling like there was something off. The most notable thing, however, was that I couldn't find Devlin. After the cake cutting and eating, he had disappeared. The guests began to leave and people began helping clean off the tables. I chatted briefly with a few people here and there, trying to figure out where he might be, so we could be on our way. Eventually, with nothing to do but stand around feeling awkward, I started helping clear off the tables too. Someone stopped me, telling me that wasn't my job, that I was supposed to leave. Leave where? My groom had disappeared! There was no grand exit surrounded by scattered rice or floating bubbles. Just awkwardness.

When he finally sauntered into the reception hall, I grabbed his hand and started pulling him toward the exit.

"Let's go."

He was slow to agree, glancing around at the decorations

being dismantled. I pulled him towards the door and climbed in the driver's seat of my car, which some enthusiastic soul had decorated with toilet paper. I started the ignition, but he didn't get in. He told me he had to go do something first, and disappeared again. I sat there, idling, for another 10 minutes. Finally, I got out to look for him, again.

"What's going on?"

"Nothing."

"Can we GO, please?"

"Yeah, sure, we can go."

"What are you doing? Why is it taking so long to get out of here?"

He climbed in the car, ignoring my question. I restarted the car and we got about one minute down the road before he said "I really needed to do something before I left. Can you please turn around? It's important."

Fed up, I didn't say a word. I turned the car around, pulled into a parking space, and emotionally disengaged from him. This is how it would always be. Slightly-off behavior. Vague answers, or no answer at all. Nothing alarming enough that made me put my foot down and demand clarity (I wouldn't get it anyway), just things he would find a way to "reason away" or distract me from.

Eventually we headed down the highway towards our hotel. Devlin spoke first.

"We need to head to the airport."

"What?!"

"Joe is at the airport where he rented the bridal party car. We need to pick him up and take him to Adela and Radu's hotel room tonight. He is going to stay with them."

You have got to be kidding. After all this, now we get to play taxi for everyone else?

Oh, but he wasn't joking. We spent our wedding night picking Joe up and playing taxi for him to get to the hotel where he would sleep that night. We arrived at Adela and Radu's room and spent another hour there with Devlin's friends, who were basically strangers to me, making awkward small talk while pretending we had known each other forever. My "off-feeling" intensified.

I had no way of knowing our wedding would mark the day Devlin flipped a switch. The trophy - me - had been won; the prize obtained. The challenge of the chase was over and now the dynamics changed overnight. My worth in his eyes was diminishing by the hour, and so were my freedoms. I had missed the red flags.

6

EARLY LESSONS

Right from the beginning, Devlin started the control tactics, but I would be unaware of it for years. It didn't occur to me that he had ulterior motives. Despite his strange behaviors that left me confused, I had no reason to believe he had a hidden agenda. I believed he loved me.

The first tactic he used was isolation.

Then covertly punishing me when I didn't conform to his ideals.

Blaming me.

Insinuating I was dumb.

Vague threats.

Withdrawing affection.

Ever-changing expectations.

I thought it was *my* fault. Score #1. Devlin: 1, Me: 0. I never viewed marriage as a game to keep score, but it must have been one for him. He would win big.

Our first order of business was moving in together. Since we had lived on opposite sides of the country, it took a few road trips to get all of our belongings to Savannah, Georgia where he had decided we should start our new life. We had no friends or family there. His claim before the wedding was that he was missionary-minded and wanted to start a new church group in a place where there was not already an established one. It sounded pious and adventurous, though I was not much of an adventurer. Still, if this was important to him, I was supportive. We were merging lives and goals - we would work together as a team. Isolation: Score #2.

He flew to California, where his apartment was, a week before me so that he could pack his stuff, and instructed me to find a flight for myself. I would fly there later to help him drive both his vehicles from California to Georgia. The road trip took a week, and was very unhappy.

Desertion was the next weapon of choice. When we stopped at a rest area in the desert of Arizona, I returned from the bathroom only to find out Devlin's vehicle was gone. This was odd. I waited, asking random people if I could borrow their cell phone to call him, but nobody wanted to do that. So I waited longer, expecting that surely Devlin would show up eventually. An entire hour passed and Devlin did not come. Something was not right. I got in my car and decided to travel to the next exit, hoping to find a pay phone of some sort. I had no cell phone and no map. I had no idea where I was, or how far I would need to go.

Desert exits are far away from each other. I drove for a long time before I got to the first one, and right before reaching it I saw his van pulled off on the shoulder. I pulled off too. He was irritated, wondering why I had taken so long to catch up.

"Why did you even leave? I had no idea where you were or why you would have gone on without me…I figured if you left, then turned around to come back to the rest area, if I had left too, you would have missed me…. Why is this my fault?"

He started spewing. "The honeybees on the trailer started

coming out of the hives. I had to leave! You should have *figured* something happened and just tried to catch up. You have to use your brain. I can't do the thinking for you all the time!"

Yet that was *exactly* what he wanted to do - *my* thinking. My thinking must always reflect his. His sermonizing would soon make sure of that.

Well, he did have the honeybees. Maybe I am over-reacting. He had a good reason to leave. It's not a big deal.

Next, Devlin didn't like how I drove - he was used to going 90 miles an hour, and my 75 miles per hour was "too slow." We would "never" get to our destination if I didn't hurry up. After fussing at me at each gas fill-up, he decided to just drive fast and leave me to eventually "catch up." I drove hundreds of miles, solo, without his van in sight, wondering when he would calm down enough for us to travel together… again, with no map or cell phone. I blindly drove on.

One incident at a time, I was learning that he marched to the beat of his own drum, and I would be left behind if I didn't change. Because I loved him, I would have to adjust.

Isn't that what all married couples do? Adjust?

I would put my hurt feelings aside, forgive, and acclimate to these new dynamics.

Isn't that what a Christian is supposed to do?

After we had moved into our new house, Devlin went out to find construction jobs for work. He had quit his job as church leader in California just prior to our wedding, over what he called "a lack of standards" they had. He had decided to return to being self-employed and do construction work. He visited hotels and asked if they needed remodeling done; many of them did. He started working within a week or so - long hours. He would leave the house at 6 a.m. and would not return until 11 p.m. to 1 o'clock in the morning. The hotels were open all night and he could paint silently in the rooms that had been sectioned off for remodeling. He said he worked so long because he needed to establish some good jobs and a good reputation in this new city. I missed him, but rationalized that the pressure of providing for a new wife must be stressing him out, so I said very little.

I felt alone and sad, in a new city, without any family or friends around, and very isolated. I tried to find a job, but found out I was pregnant six weeks after getting married, and the severe nausea prevented any more job hunting; I was really sick.

A few months passed, but his work hours did not level out. I brought up the subject a couple times but he insisted he had to work that much. Eventually we had an argument and I started crying. This made him snap.

"You *stop* that crying or *I will give you something to cry about!*"

I stopped. He had hit a nerve. A nerve that went down my spine and all the way back to childhood. I knew a threat when I heard it; I had learned well. And I knew he meant it.

I had to learn to accommodate him, had to learn to not upset him. If I wanted my needs met, his needs would have to come first. I didn't understand why he never wanted to be around me, but I would become a "good wife" - one that he would yearn to spend time with.

So I cooked. I cleaned. I ran his errands. Took care of paying the bills. Ran the secretarial part of his business. Cooked more. Cooking was extremely important in his culture, or at least that's how he presented it. I learned how to make his favorite (time-consuming!) foods, which he would devour in a matter of minutes - but it was a labor of love, right? I cooked for his family and friends that stayed with us, and even for employees that he hired to work with him. He "didn't want to eat food without inviting them to have the same," so he wanted me to make enough food for 6 or 7 adults for every meal, and deliver it to his work site. Then I would wait until they finished eating, gather up the dishes, and bring them back home.

Despite that, the food arguments began. According to him, my cooking wasn't right. Even though I made everything from scratch like he wanted, and he had loved it before we got married, he now had standards that apparently I couldn't meet. Bread was one of them. Romanians eat bread at every meal. If there is no bread, regardless what else is on the table, there is no "real food."

So I baked. Twelve loaves of bread a week, to be exact, by hand. God forbid that in my tired, pregnant state, I forget the salt, or it didn't rise well, or it was too heavy. There are so many variables to bread which I could not control, and it made him angry.

He made jokes about how I cooked. He didn't like my rice - I didn't make it the right "Romanian way" with peppers and onions and mushrooms. He laughed and made jokes about how our eyes were going to change shape and we would become oriental from "eating so much rice."

Crockpot food was off limits. He thought it was the "lazy" way to make food and said everything turned out "too mushy." However, if I made food in the crockpot and transferred it to another bowl before serving and he never knew about it, he thought it was just fine. He wanted to make sure I was spending enough time going through the motions of cooking, because that was what made it acceptable. Garlic should be shredded on a miniature shredder, or diced to minuscule pieces with a knife. A garlic press (which took a few seconds), he insisted, made it "taste different," and he didn't like it.

In little ways, he picked away at my confidence and self-worth and made me feel like my opinions and thoughts were wrong and that I couldn't do anything right. It doesn't take much to crush the spirit of a people-pleaser, and I was one. I craved validation from him, as I had received virtually none from my parents and family growing up. I wanted - no, *needed* - his approval. That made his job all the more easy. For years all it took for him to change my behavior was a look. A frown. Him turning away and ignoring me.

During our divorce years later, someone asked me "Did he ever hit you?" No, he didn't. He never needed to *because I was always compliant*. He had a weapon that worked better on me than his fist ever could, and I had handed him that weapon at the beginning of our relationship. In a moment of connection with him, I had relayed my fear of abandonment.

Bingo.

Once an abuser knows your weakness, he will use it to his greatest advantage; and Devlin did. Every time I did something he didn't like, he became silent. He would withdraw, emotionally cutting me off for days, neither looking at me or interacting. He would work longer hours at his job, avoiding answering my calls. To someone with abandonment anxiety, vulnerable and pregnant, it is a very effective threat. It did not take long for him to have complete compliance from me.

During that first year, my sister came to visit for two days. We were spending time laughing, watching a movie and folding the laundry. Devlin came home in the middle of the day, unannounced. I saw the look. *That* look. It spoke volumes of the price I would pay for "sitting around doing nothing" during the day, instead of working hard. Company was not a reason to relax. I jumped up and started putting away the laundry that was already folded.

See? I am not just relaxing. I am actively working. Please, notice this.

He glanced at the television. I pretended I didn't know what was happening on the screen. It was just something *my sister* was watching. Yeah, that. I folded a few more outfits and took them to the dresser.

Actively working. I'm active. I'm not "wasting time."

It was no use. He had already decided to be mad. He uttered a few words to my sister in the voice he used when he was pretending to be polite, but was angry inside. I caught the tone.

Crap!

Sure enough, he withdrew that night, and the atmosphere in the house was edgy. I made extra food, hoping to appease. I think that served to only strengthen his sense of entitlement. I would never win the power struggle. Gradually. Stealthily. Almost imperceptibly. This is how he gained control. Little by little, comment by comment, one *look* at a time, he changed my beliefs to match his.

I am sure to people on the outside, it would have been apparent that these were irrational things to be upset about. But when you are in a relationship, you are too emotionally involved to recognize it for what it is. I believed he cared about me, and never once imagined that he would deliberately do anything to hurt me. People who love you do not intentionally wound, after all; they don't play mind games. The reality of the situation was not even on my radar.

Maybe I just didn't understand.

This is when he started to get inside my head. This is when the mental tapes - that would play in loops in my mind for years to come - began.

I started doubting myself.

If I could just...then he wouldn't get mad.

If I was just more...then he would be happy.

If I remembered to never... then we could have marital harmony.

I essentially took on managing his emotions. I avoided doing anything that would trigger his displeasure, and tried to make sure that his world was as perfect as possible. I had been taught a lie that I was personally responsible for other people's feelings and actions because I had "influence." The church had twisted the concept of "positive influence" into error by teaching *I* was the ultimate factor in whether or not things worked out – that it was all up to me. If I changed *me*, then we would both be happy. That lie built the foundation for everything that was to come.

7

DECEPTION

I don't know how many years we were married before I saw his fake passport. I have a memory of finding it under our bed in a large box filled with all kinds of random stuff. The passport was just thrown in there, well-hidden amongst common things.

I flipped through the pages and compared the pictures. His particular kind of passport required two identical photos - one in the front of the book and one in the back. Although the men in the pictures shared similar facial features, it was obviously *not* the same person. It looked like a real botch job - even the lamination had wrinkles in it.

How in the world did he get through the border with this?

It was only after our engagement that Devlin told me he had initially come to the U.S. illegally. I was shocked. I was also 20 years old and didn't understand the true significance of this piece of news. I knew people who had crossed the border illegally and had heard their stories. They had gone through the process to become citizens as refugees. What I didn't know about Devlin, however, was that he continued to be illegal, and had no intention of doing anything about it.

Before we met, he was living and working in the U.S. - for years - under the radar. Eventually, when he was offered a job working for the church, they applied for a work visa for him, and for a short period of time it seemed possible for him to begin the process to obtain a green card. That all came to a stop when he quit the job right before we got married. Of course, he didn't tell *me* any of this. He only told me the parts that sounded good. "The church got me a work visa and my attorney is taking care of stuff" is the version I got.

The initial story of how he arrived here sounded fairly benign. He despised the prior communistic regime he had grown up in in Romania and was intent on leaving it all behind. He talked about making plans with a friend to leave his country. They traveled to Spain and he eventually flew to America. He talked about starting a new life here and how he moved in with friends near Atlanta, Georgia. There was a large Romanian community there that helped him find work and survive. It almost sounded idealistic - leaving the old for the new, leaving the broken behind for a new beginning, while going through a difficult struggle to obtain it. A story of overcoming.

The rest of the story came out later: He had been involved with an organized crime ring that was involved with three countries. He paid them $1500 to obtain a fake passport, which was a lot of money in Romania at the time. He hid his real passport on the inside of a sandwich in a small plastic bag (because all possessions were searched at the borders) so that he wouldn't get caught having two of them. Upon arriving at the international airport in Atlanta, he presented the fake one and was accepted through customs. His friends gave him a place to stay and information on how to get more fake identification that he would need here in the U.S. - a false social security card and driver's license. He moved to Michigan with "friends of friends" for a short period of time so he could receive mail at their place and "prove" residency. Michigan was one of the easiest places to get a driver's license since at that time they didn't ask for citizenship papers.

Over time, as more parts of the story came out, I realized the gravity of the situation. When we first got married, I had no idea that he could be arrested and deported at any time. It soon became a source of high stress for me. He was the only one bringing in an income, and for the entire duration of our marriage he refused to put aside any money for savings. If he was suddenly picked up by U.S. immigration officers, I would be homeless with four little kids.

∽

"Hey, are you busy?

"Not really. What's up?"

"I need help."

"What's going on?"

"I...I don't even know how to explain this...I found papers."

"What kind of papers?"

"I'm going through my file box and I'm finding all this... stuff! Just random stuff! Car registration papers where Devlin forged my name...A car bill of sale where he used my driver's license number and information to buy it - where did he get my license number? We weren't even living together then! He forged numbers on this other paper to evade taxes - also in my name. There's a bank statement where he lied that he was a citizen to open an account, and he closed out our joint account. Our tax papers show that he made $40,000 more than usual, but he wasn't paying the bills - I was. Where did $40,000 disappear to? This is money I never even knew about!" I rambled on.

After I had filed for divorce, my friend became used to

hearing random weirdness from me. The divorce turned my life on its head. Some weeks were just a blur of emotions and exhaustion. There were times it felt as if there was a short break in the clouds, where it seemed life was starting to stabilize, only to again become a blurry world as new information was revealed. He had lived a secret life.

I was mostly in confusion. It felt futile - trying to piece together a puzzle with most of the pieces missing. I was trying to figure out the storyline of a whole other life he lived that I knew nothing of. It is extremely rattling to find out that the person you thought you knew for almost half your life was actually lying to you about everything - *everything!* - from day one.

I dreaded picking up the mail. Every time I got an envelope from my attorney my heart started racing.

My friend got another call.

"New dynamic. Devlin's interrogatories say that he has borrowed tens of thousands of dollars."

"What's an interrogatory?"

"It's like a question-and-answer type document from my attorney. Devlin has to answer the questions truthfully under penalty of perjury. It's like being interrogated, but in writing instead of verbally."

"So then... what?"

"First of all, he has another fake address on the other side of the country. When asked about his expenses, he says he owes his brother $10,000, and some random friend from his church - that he is not really friends with - he owes him $10,000 too! That's in addition to the tens of thousands he owes in credit card debt. Then he admitted he made over $100,000 from one client! What is he doing with all this money?!"

"Is he getting more fake documentation?"

"I don't know. I already thought of that. Fake documents

to get four kids out of the country is probably pretty expensive. I can't even think about it...."

I thought back to the arguments about our kids. Devlin continually used them as pawns in his game to control me. If there was something that I did that angered him, he would find a way to punish me by using the kids.

"How would you like it if I took the kids and you never saw them again?"

The words echoed in my head, again and again, and ultimately kept me compliant with his wishes. I knew he was capable of doing it.

"If I ever had to leave the country, I would find a way to come back. But if there was some reason I couldn't, I would travel to Canada, Spain, or Australia...."

Totally strange conversations. Devlin specialized in vague and hypothetical situations that didn't make any sense. I thought back to the time we got the children passports. Devlin was insistent we have them "just in case" of an emergency scenario.

"In an emergency," he argued, "you can't wait 6 weeks for them to be processed."

He never mentioned what sort of emergency would qualify for a trip out of the country. I thought it was a bit weird. He had no intention of going back to Romania to visit family - or visiting anywhere outside the U.S. for that matter - because he wouldn't be able to get back across the border. Leaving the country meant leaving permanently. If you do it legally, that is.

Over the years he hired illegal immigrants to help him with construction work. During lunch they would have conversations about how they got through the border. Devlin told me tidbits of their stories once. He never really explained the whole story though. He had this weird circular way of talking, in which he would explain half of a story, and leave the rest of it for speculation.

I think this is what fueled a lot of fear over the years. He told me "just enough" but "not enough." He effectually planted seeds to let me know what he was capable of doing, without making a direct statement of what he was actually going to do. I am not sure if this stemmed from being raised under communism (where it was a way of life to avoid answering questions, and to never say anything that can be used against you in a court of law) or if it was just his innate abusive personality, but he was very consistent at avoiding direct statements. When asked a question, first he would try to answer with sentences that could be understood in more than one way. If pressed for further clarification, he would answer the question with a question of his own (a form of deflecting), or would change the trajectory completely. It was absolutely brain-bending to listen to.

I remembered the times we were leaving our house in Savannah. We had a long sandy driveway that dead-ended into a gravel road. At the end of our driveway Devlin got out of the car and raked over the sand. He flung the rake into the bushes, got back in the car, and smiled triumphantly.

"Now we will be able to see if someone drives in while we are gone."

Who does this stuff? This is paranoid and crazy.

It was exactly this kind of behavior that made me realize he had different thought processes than a typical person. Subconsciously, it also registered with me that if I ever ended up on his "bad side," all his paranoid or abnormal behaviors would be directed against me - to stalk me, harm me, or to "get even."

It's funny the things our minds take note of, which come to mind years later. And then we realize *"I always knew it…."*

8

LET THE GAMES BEGIN

I loved my Isuzu Rodeo. I think it was mainly because the back hatch swung open like a door, instead of lifting up - it made dealing with groceries so much easier. I didn't have to duck down in the car to put the baby in her car seat - it was the perfect height. It was little things in life like this that made me happy.

I should have disguised my delight. As soon as Devlin discovered how much I liked it, he sold it. In less than two weeks, it was gone. I was unaware of his game. I was, however, disappointed, and had a strange feeling rise up inside me when he would do this. Although I didn't have the conscious thoughts at that time, my heart had noticed the pattern that every time I liked something, Devlin would eliminate it. Sometimes it takes awhile for your mind to catch up with what your heart already knows. Back then I thought he loved me, so I didn't put a sinister motive to his actions.

Ha ha.

My first vehicle was also gone in a week. I was confused. It was a silver Nissan that Devlin had bought for me as a gift. I had thought I was going to keep it for many years. But not long after we settled into our new home, he told me to clean it out very well.

I felt embarrassed. I didn't think the car was that messy. I didn't want my new husband thinking I was a slob. I lowered my eyes, unsure what to say. I didn't need to say anything, as he continued on.

"I want to sell it."

"What?! Why?"

"I want to get you a better one."

"Why, what's wrong with this one? I love it!"

"It's just not what I'm thinking you need. I really like the Mercedes station wagons. They are made in Germany and are solid vehicles. They are engineered so much better...."

He continued talking. I tried to make sense of what he was saying, but something felt off. As he talked, I noted the words he used. This was not up for debate - I didn't have a say about the car. *He wasn't asking.* He put a "For Sale" ad in the paper that day. My car was gone in 3 days.

I didn't get a say in what vehicle we got next. Or the next. There were no conversations or mutual decisions, no consideration of what I liked. He wanted a Mercedes. I would be crazy to complain about that as far as name brand goes, except the Mercedes he got was old, from an auction, and had major problems that he promised to fix (but never did).

He moved on to regulating my personal life. When my friends would call, he would answer the phone and hang up on them. When they would leave messages, he would get angry about how "immature" the messages were and then withdraw attention from me for several hours. This was his way of showing displeasure. Then the people started coming.

About six weeks after we married, his mother came from Romania. I was excited for him - he had not seen her in seven years. But I don't think I was prepared for her to stay for six months. Neither was I prepared for the cultural mindset

Romanians had - where people come to live with you long term.

His Romanian friend joined us a few months later - and also stayed for six months. Then his brother; another six months. For the first year of our marriage, I basically ran a bed and breakfast for people who did not speak my language. I spent my days cooking and cleaning up after them. At first, I did it cheerfully, wanting to please him, and them. But as the months passed, I became increasingly frustrated. Transitioning to married life by ourselves would have been challenging enough, but now I was pregnant with our first baby and spent many days in bed, too nauseated to move. I vomited continually and could barely hold down water. Running a hotel service for people I could not even communicate with was wearing me out. We had no privacy. I felt like I lived in a fishbowl.

Bringing it up was a mistake. He attacked. He told me I should feel grateful - that housing people was "an honor," and that typical American hospitality was a disgrace. After all, people in Romania had "nothing," yet opened their homes to people for *years*. This was my opportunity to show love to people and I should be happy about it. I was made out to be selfish; my frustrations were dismissed. Fishbowl life would continue whether I liked it or not.

Everything that happened could be explained "reasonably" at first. Devlin had a rationale for why he said or did virtually anything. Also, he chose "small" issues to pick away at - the things that "were not a big deal." Why would I argue with him about "such nonessential" things?

Finances were one example. He started using my credit card before we got married, but it was to purchase things for *our* wedding. "The least I could do" was give him access to an account we were going to share in a few months anyway, I thought. It was *our* debt and we would be paying it off together (except that never happened). It was *reasonable* to do this.

After we got married, we opened a bank account in both our names. He was the only one working. When he completed a job and got a check from his customer, he would cash it at their bank and only deposit in our account what he thought I should spend for bills and groceries. He kept the rest as cash for himself because "That's what we did in Romania - used cash." For thirteen years I never knew how much he had, or what he spent it on. But it was *reasonable* for him to continue something he had done his whole life, right?

It wasn't a big deal, after all.

Once in a while he would hand me $100 and I would ask what it was for. He said, "For whatever you need to buy." It was "kind" of him to do this, but it was also the beginning of my "allowance" - and the end of my control of our money.

Our spending and saving habits were the opposite of each other, which is common in marriage, but we did not just disagree on how to spend money; rather he slowly gained control of *all* the money. While I would visit several stores to find the best prices for groceries and small items, he would impulse buy items worth hundreds, if not thousands, of dollars without ever asking for my input. One day he brought home an $800 tile saw that he decided was necessary for his business. Another time it was a new lawnmower he paid $1000 for. Then a used car he spent a few thousand on. He also brought home a custom-built front door he had paid $1000 for, with the intent to resell it since "the original owner probably paid $5000 for it." (The door sat out in the weather and rotted away for the next 11 years)

We never made "mutually agreeable" financial decisions.

This felt very disrespectful to me, but he acted like it should be "normal." He made the money, after all.

In order for him to afford his impulse buys, however, my daily life had to be affected and he wanted new dynamics; he wanted *me* to stop wasting our resources. Putting clothes into the dryer was "wasteful" to him. After all, people in Romania didn't do that! I was aware how much electricity our appliances used, and I usually hung the clothes outside on a clothesline. But for a few weeks during the spring, the pollen was so bad it would leave a thick film of yellow on the cars, deck, lawn furniture, and also the laundry. I had such severe seasonal allergies that my nose was raw and bloody and my lungs felt like they were full of fluid. I was blamed for wasting money and resources if I dried clothes or towels in the dryer during those weeks to keep them from being covered in pollen. He thought that if I just "drank more carrot juice" and "ate more garlic," that my immune system could handle the pollen and I could stop wasting money.

I was also taught not to spend any money from our joint account - I might overdraw the account because he was the only one who knew what checks he had written. Money flowed in and out without my knowledge or consent, and I never knew if the balance was accurate or not. When I asked him about our financial status, he would talk in circles about the jobs he was doing - and would be doing in the future - but never answered the question about our bottom line.

Not being financially stable put a lot of stress on me. Devlin didn't want me to have a job - we had decided that I would stay home with the kids - so I couldn't improve our income. He refused to put any money aside for savings. We lived paycheck to paycheck - not because we had to, but because of his impulsive habits. If we had money, he would spend it. I was continually worried about the possibility of him being picked up by immigration if he happened to be pulled over for a traffic violation and they figured out he was illegal. I would have absolutely no way to pay the bills or provide for our kids - no backup at all. So I did something that made him angry. I started saving money.

I didn't know it would make him angry. I thought it would be helpful one day if we ever had an emergency. Every time he gave me my "allowance" I would put aside five or ten dollars to save. I kept it in the closet in a box disguised as a book. I didn't tell him about it; I just saved it up over time. Then one day he came home frazzled. There was an important bill due that day, and he didn't have the money to pay it. He was talking to me, and to himself, about how he expected a check for a job, but now couldn't get it for another day or two. I eventually went into the closet and returned with enough money to pay the bill. He was stunned.

It wasn't a good version of stunned. The shocked look on his face revealed something else - he felt I had betrayed him by hiding money. He became real calm all of a sudden - the way he always did when he was mad - yet he spoke nice words and took the money from my hand. There was no thank you or appreciation, just logistical talk about how he needed to run into town now and pay the bill. He acted relieved but disturbed. I had been deceitful in his eyes.

Another area of manipulation was food. He would buy expensive foods for himself, like specialty olives and dates from ethnic stores, and bring them home, insisting I try them because I would like them. If I didn't, he acted surprised, in a disapproving way, as if there was something strangely wrong with his wife for not sharing his tastes. "That's okay, once you get used to them, you will like them. You know, they are much healthier than the ones at the grocery store - those are so flavorless and full of chemicals. These are so much better…" The implication was that surely nobody intelligent would choose bland and poisoned food over something "better and healthier" - that wouldn't be *reasonable*. A slow process of eliminating my preferences began. Later, he would insist I get rid of groceries I bought if they had ingredients he didn't approve of.

Then there were his comments about "a better way" to do almost anything I needed to do. They were just "suggestions" he said. He wasn't *telling* me what to do, he just thought if I did it his way, it would make my jobs so much easier. That's *reasonable*, isn't it?

He was only looking out for my best interest, right?

No. No, he wasn't. He really wanted to micromanage my life and have my ways of doing things conform perfectly to his will. The issues were brought up again and again and he would emotionally withdraw, or act hurt and insulted, if I didn't enthusiastically embrace his ideas. Sometimes it was very subtle, but he was good at relaying the message that I was out of line. As time passed it would become harder and harder to stay within his lines.

9

DEVALUATION

I answered the door, and was met with a bright bouquet of pink carnations and baby's breath.

"Hey! These are for you."

I took the flowers, quizzically, and he continued, "Just because you are special!"

Devlin set his cooler and jacket down on the floor and gave me a big hug and a kiss.

"How was your day?"

My day had been fine. I was glad he was home earlier than normal.

"We finished up the job at work a little earlier, so I thought I would come home sooner and work on my van. The brakes need a little help because I've been carrying a lot of heavy tools lately…"

He continued talking while he took off his work boots and went into the bathroom to wash his hands. I could hear him clearly over the water splashing in the sink, but I didn't really take in what he said. I looked down at the flowers.

I felt a strange mix of happiness and disappointment; happy because he was home sooner but sad because he made it clear he wouldn't be spending that extra time with us - just his vehicle. It was such a quick feeling - there one minute and gone the next. I had learned to brush off disappointment from him so fast it was as if it almost didn't exist. I should have been used to it by then anyway, but somehow I never was. The little glimmer of hope deep inside me always burned, no matter how many times it was blown out. Hope that one day he would want to spend time with *me*.

It's not like there were not any good times at all. It was the good times that kept me hoping that one day all this would change. One day when we had more money, he could work less and spend more time with our family. One day, after we bought a house...after he sold another vehicle...after he got his priorities straightened out...after we didn't have other people living in our house... then we could start living a better life.

Besides, there was that time that he took an hour break from work in the middle of the day when he had a job on the island, and we took the kids for a walk on the beach. And that time we had a picnic in the park between two job sites he had to visit that day. These times were extremely spread out - only once or twice a year, but it kept me believing the lie: One day this will get better.

It is hard for people who have not experienced the descent into domestic violence, to really understand the dynamics that play out, and why the victim cannot just "put her foot down," stand up to her abuser, and demand change.

What happens on a daily basis is a strange mix of devaluation and humiliation of the victim, as the abuser ascends to "ruler." His will becomes sovereign. In between that, is mixed good experiences and happy moments. The evil is interlaced with a few fun times and warm fuzzy feelings. These are what keep you holding onto the relationship, and give you hope that things will get better. You don't believe you are abused, because if that were true, surely it would be bad *all* the time...right? You are told you are the problem. Even when you do put your foot down, your will is dominated and intentionally disregarded. You are taught no matter what, you won't win. Putting your foot down never accomplishes anything but making your abuser angry and causing fallout for you. You eventually just stop trying.

One example was the birth of our first baby - an experience that should be joyful and anticipated. I had wanted a home birth with a midwife, but it didn't pan out - Georgia state law forbade midwives from attending home births. I was terrified of the hospital. I had heard stories of unnecessary Cesarean sections, botched epidurals resulting in lung failure of mothers, damage to babies. It scared me. I was also 20 years old and over-confident - I thought I could just "do it by myself." So we planned an unassisted birth at home. This suited Devlin just fine. The less people around, the better. He was already working effectively on his mission to isolate me, one interaction at a time. This would be a good opportunity for him.

Labor began in the early morning hours on a Saturday. Our daughter came a week before her due date. We had invited some new friends, originally from Hungary, to come over for lunch after their church service. We had met the family only twice. They had three teenage children. By the time they arrived, I had been having contractions for 9 hours already. Devlin told them I "wasn't feeling well and was laying down in the bedroom." They spent the next four hours with him, laughing in the dining room, eating stuffed shells, salad, and bread, and telling stories in Hungarian. Devlin checked on me a few times and finally asked if I would come out and say hi to everyone.

By that time I was really struggling - exhausted, in pain. I knelt on the bathroom floor, half naked, trying to remember to not grit my teeth when the pain hit. I waved him off; I hurt too much to talk. He left.

For 13 hours I had labored alone. There were no signs of infant distress, but I was getting tired. I crawled up on the bed and closed my eyes.

How much longer? I can't do this anymore.

There was a knock at the door. Devlin came in.

Since when does he knock?

"Nora wants to see you."

"What?!"

"Nora figured out that you are in labor and she wants to check on you, to make sure you are okay. I told her that they probably need to leave, and we are calling the midwife, but she wants to see you."

Calling the midwife. Yeah, good luck with that.

I shake my head, my eyes squeezed shut. I am in a fog. I can't handle people now. I am half naked. This baby is on its way.

"Look, just do it anyway. I don't want her panicking. Just act like everything is okay, and then they are going to go, and it'll all be fine."

"NO!"

A contraction hits and I gasp. The pain increases and I try to hold back any sound. Apparently, this is a big secret.

Be silent!

A whimper escapes anyway. I can't help it. The pain engulfs me and I try desperately to moderate my breathing, which is supposed to help.

Devlin is unmoved by my vulnerability. He picks a

blanket up off the floor and tosses it over my back, like a saddle on a horse, trying to cover my lower body.

Then he lets Nora in the room.

I'm exposed. Vulnerable. Exhausted.

I am naked in front of a stranger, in the worst pain I've experienced yet.

Unprotected, unsupported.

Just an object.

A humiliated object.

It was times like this, that the message of worthlessness wormed its way into my soul, and spoke loud and clear to my subconscious mind. My irritation was glossed over, dismissed, as if I was crazy for expecting him to guard my privacy or preference. After all, he told me later, he only insisted "for the better good" - he wanted to palliate her so she wouldn't call 9-1-1. Everything he did was for the better good, and of course, I was not smart enough to know what was good for us.

Nora came in, chattering that it would "all be over soon," and insisting that Devlin call the midwife immediately, which he promised to do (*lie!*). Our daughter, Emma, was born on the bathroom floor later that night.

Another experience was when Devlin was at work and he called me on the phone to ask me to pick up some construction materials from the store and deliver them to him at his job, to save him some time. I reluctantly agreed, putting my whole day on hold, for his impulsive whim. While getting the children ready to go, I walked by a window. The sun was shining extremely brightly that day, and it glared off of a vehicle in the parking lot. When the light hit my eyes, something happened; I immediately could not see. I had blind spots in my vision.

They would not go away. I waited, expecting them to clear, but after about 20 minutes I called him back and told him what happened. I explained that I didn't think I should drive because I couldn't see properly. My vision was greatly impaired.

He got angry, as if it were my fault - as if I was making up a big excuse.

Nasty.

Loud.

Shaming me for being stupid.

So once again, against my better judgement, I obeyed him; got in the car, and drove - half blind - to the store, and then an hour to his job site. When I arrived at his work, he was not just pleasant, but smiling. He was pleased with me. He gave me a big hug and thanked me for going out of my way to help him, he really appreciated it. He had "such a good wife!" I had done a good job. I had obeyed.

10

THERE ARE ALWAYS REASONS

It started out "innocently" enough, at least from my end. I was too naive at the time to know the patterns of abuse that existed in our marriage. I simply didn't know what I was dealing with, and certainly had nothing to compare it to. I knew he was a workaholic and grossly neglected me and the children. I knew he would fly into rages over fairly benign things. And I knew I was miserable.

But I didn't understand the dynamic of power and control that dominated every aspect of our relationship. I didn't have the labels or education to know just how verbally and emotionally destructive he was. Like all abuse, it increased slowly over time, normalizing bad behavior and making me somewhat desensitized to it. He took away my will and opinions so slowly and strategically that I didn't know it was happening. He was creating the perfect storm, and though I felt the initial disturbing winds, no weather forecast could have predicted the hurricane of madness that would eventually erupt.

We had an ultimate goal to leave the city and move to the country where we would have plenty of space to raise the kids and expand his hobby of beekeeping into a possible business. That was the sales pitch from Devlin, anyway. Like a good salesman, he pointed out things that are true (i.e. "It would be better for the kids...") without expounding on the catch. The reality was, he needed to isolate me more. He had succeeded so far in alienating me from family and friends by blocking their phone calls and convincing me that they weren't really great friends after all, "since they never called" me.

By this time, however, I was starting to form friendships with people locally, and he didn't like it. One new friend in particular had a strong personality, and a sense that something was off. I think he feared her influence and the potential that she would eventually call him out on his behavior, or "poison" me against him. It was time to move the tent stakes.

One night he came home from work as I was hurrying to get his dinner on the table. He always came home late, so we never ate together. I would have to rewarm his food hours later. At that particular time, I had two toddlers underfoot that sucked up a good portion of my energy, and I was several months pregnant with our third baby. That night they were awake, even though it was past their bedtime. It had been days since they had seen their dad, as he left early in the morning before they woke up and got home after they were asleep for the night. So I let them stay up to catch a few minutes of "daddy time." Devlin said hello, then went to the bathroom to wash his hands which were really dirty from his work construction site. Then all hell broke loose.

He was mad about the hand towel.

Or rather the lack of one on the towel bar.

This was unforgivable in his eyes. He started ranting about how I didn't care about his needs. Saying that he didn't ask for much, and the fact that I can't "get it together" enough to make sure there is always a towel in the bathroom to wipe his hands on, proved that I was not committed to him.

I went to the bathroom. There was, in fact, a hand towel, but it had fallen off the bar and onto the floor like it did multiple times a day when our three-year-old grabbed it. Every time I was in the bathroom I was rehanging that thing.

His rant escalated into me being blamed. I was the reason we couldn't "get ahead" in life and save money. I was the one who stayed home while he worked all these crazy hours "for us!" I was blamed for all kinds of random, unrelated stuff that didn't make a whole lot of sense. But this was normal. It was not a case of the straw that broke the camel's back. It was just ridiculous rants, probably unrelated to me at all. And, as usual, he didn't stop until he had won. "Winning" meant he got me to cry or cower, or both.

After he finally got me good and upset, he went and ate his dinner, leaving me a nervous wreck in the bedroom. During these times I knew better than to confront him or make any attempt to finish the argument. Instead I cowered and stayed out of his way. He ignored me, took a shower and went to bed, leaving me to clean up the dishes and put the kids down for the night.

This hand towel "offense" caused him to give me the silent treatment for three days. He would leave for work at 5 a.m. and not return home until well after midnight. I never knew if he was "just angry" or if he had possibly gotten in an accident. He wouldn't answer my calls. He effectively stonewalled me all day and night and ignored my existence in order to punish me. After the third day I was so on edge and stressed, I figured another confrontation was better than one more day of endless tension. So while he was sleeping, I took his car keys and hid them in the closet. He would not be able to leave without being forced to at least make civil conversation. Or *something.*

This is where his craziness came out. He was so intent on not looking at, or speaking to, me that the next morning he went out to his vehicle and spent an entire hour dismantling his ignition switch and trying to hot wire the car so he could start it without the keys. It was a whole new level of foolishness.

I don't remember the exact conversation we had when he finally decided to confront me again, or how many days later it was, but I know it consisted of him threatening to leave me unless I "got on board" with his dreams and goals in life. I would need to "be on the same page" with whatever he wanted. He said we needed to move. That was the next goal. He told me to go online and look up properties for sale and map out where they were. He told me to look up house plans and blueprints and find something within our budget. Then he told me to plan a two-week road trip to "go find property to buy." His plan was to build a house on it himself.

Within a month we were taking a road trip. We traveled up to northern Georgia and into Tennessee, looking at properties along the way. I was extremely tired from the elevation change and from being pregnant. I could barely stay awake. In addition, I was bleeding, significantly. I was afraid I was miscarrying the baby.

Looking back, I see it for the craziness it was. But back then, a doctor was not an option with him. Neither was being "sidetracked" from his mission by a potential miscarriage. I was left to myself to worry and mitigate it the best I could.

I tried hard to appease him. When he complained that I should stay awake to "see the scenery" because "we are on this road trip for *you*, after all," I forced my eyes open. When he told me to get out of the car and look at the properties, I obeyed. The only time I put my foot down was when he said I needed to hike around the five acres of one property to determine its worth. Seriously?! I should have been home on bedrest with medical care. Instead, I sat in the car and reclined the passenger seat as far back as it would go, praying the bleeding would stop.

We eventually found a property that he liked. While I had my own opinions, I was too tired and stressed to really care at that point. I knew my opinion didn't matter anyway. After he looked at the property, he decided we should put an offer down on it, right then and there. I was incredulous.

"Shouldn't we at least sleep on it? Or maybe think about it more than just an hour?"

"Did we come here to buy property or did we not? Why are we taking this trip? For some vacation?" He spit out the word "vacation" as if it was a nasty, bitter food.

I wasn't overly impressed with the property. It showed signs of poor drainage and possibly wetlands. It didn't have road access. We would have to drive our vehicle over very damp and muddy ground to even get to it. The seller had been trying to get rid of it for a long time without success.

But as the "good obedient wife," I thought it was my duty to be compliant. I also felt if I went along (again!) with what he wanted, he would calm down and drop the threat of leaving us. He would be happy if he achieved the first step of his goal and somehow it would all work out. Little did I know, that decision would almost cost my life. The nightmare had begun.

11

THE SHED AND THE LIE

We moved into the shed in April. By then, the baby had been born and Devlin had finished up the major construction jobs he had been working on. Our loose ends in Savannah had been tied up and it was time to finally move on. The first trip to Tennessee Devlin made on his own, hauling behind his vehicle the "workshop trailer" - the first shed we would live in.

Devlin had built it for himself as a place to work on his beekeeping hobby and store a few tools. He built it on a 6 x 10-foot trailer and constructed it out of leftover materials from his construction business. It had four walls, two doors, and two windows. A work-bench platform reached from one wall to another on the furthest end.

When we moved into it, he put a small cabinet inside. This gave us one drawer, a platform for a jug of water, and a small shelf to hold a few cups. There was shelving behind the door to hold his tools and some cans of food. A mattress went on the floor to sleep. Between all this, and the fact that the door swung inwards, we only really had 2 square feet to move around, or 6 square feet if the door was closed. This would be all the living space we would have for us and our three small children for several months.

When Devlin originally articulated his plans to me about building our own house, it had never included living in a shed. He had portrayed the whole event as a fairly simple process.

"It will only take me about two weeks to put up the main frame of the house. Then we can live inside of it and finish it a little at a time. It won't be fancy, but we will have our own place and will get it pulled together very quickly. We can save money and make head-way a lot faster than paying rent somewhere else *and* trying to fund building."

Although I was not excited about the idea, surely I could "camp" for a few weeks. A lot of people do that for fun. We could certainly do it to achieve a goal that was much greater than a vacation.

The thing I remember most was the cold. The temperatures that year were still dipping down into the 40s at night. The two girls slept on the work bench on top of several folded blankets. Devlin and I slept on the floor with the baby between us. The floor was uninsulated. It took several weeks before he brought in the 2-inch thick mattress which he got from a hotel that was throwing it away. At that point, I didn't care about the potential germ issue that it might bring with it - anything was better than the hard, freezing wood. Prior to the mattress, we were sleeping on top of some cut up cardboard boxes Devlin had laid on the floor. We spread a few blankets on top of them to sleep on. It wasn't enough. My back and head froze all night. So did my face. I would continually wake up, trying to figure out another way to get warm. I would wrap anything around myself - even a scarf around my back - in hopes that it would help. I dressed the girls in three sets of pajamas and woke up several times a night to check on them and make sure they stayed covered with blankets. The baby got the same treatment with the addition of being wrapped in my extreme-weather down-filled coat. He slept peacefully and toasty. We all wore hats to bed. I woke up tired and achy from the hard floor and from the cold. I prayed for warmer weather.

Devlin's first order of business was building a second shed to hold all of our belongings which were brought to Tennessee on his work trailer. He refused to spend money on a moving van or storage unit. Instead, he had rigged up a way to connect his construction scaffolding bars to the trailer, loaded it with boxes and furniture, and then slid a few pieces of plywood between our stuff and the bars, creating "walls" to hold everything on the trailer. He topped it off with a few tarps and proclaimed it road-ready. It was not weather-ready however, and our things were being destroyed by rain. He needed to build another shed for our stuff.

He built the second shed out of leftover scrap material from past construction jobs and bought the sheet metal for the roof. On the back of this shed he made an overhang under which he would build the "outhouse."

The outhouse was just three plywood walls underneath the overhanging sheet metal roof. A rough bench, also made from plywood, was inside. There was a hole cut out in the middle of the bench under which he placed a five-gallon bucket. This would be our "toilet" for the next 2-1/2 years. Once or twice a week, the bucket would be emptied into a large hole that Devlin dug out close to the creek.

This was the job I hated the most - emptying the poop bucket. It was heavy and filled with sewage and creatures. I am not even sure what kind of creatures they were, but the bucket was living, moving, squirming at all times. The maggots inside were over an inch long and 1/4-inch thick. We only used the bucket when we couldn't hold ourselves anymore. Usually we chose to pee in the grass or leaves behind the shed because it felt better than to catch a glimpse of the squirming poop slurry. The smell was nauseating. I always thought I was going to throw up if one of those worms somehow escaped and crawled on my bottom or leg when I was using the "toilet." I shudder even thinking about it.

For the first 6 weeks Devlin was on the property, building sheds, or in town trying to drum up new construction business. After the second shed was up and filled with stuff, he began a third shed which was going to be a "temporary living space" for us while we built our "real" house on the other side of the property. This shed would eventually turn into his beekeeping business, he said, where he planned to extract honey and build beehives. Those were his ambitions, anyway.

I think his real goal was to just have us living in little sheds in the jungle of weeds forever. Nothing ever transpired to build a house. The sheds deteriorated and became nothing but warped, rotted plywood. A fire hazard. Filled with rats.

We ended up living in the 6 x 10-foot shed for 4 more months. But this time it was just me and the kids. In June, Devlin left us there to survive on our own. He went back to Savannah to work because by this time he had spent all of our money - we only had $30 left to our name. He said he would be back in a few weeks.

I don't remember what I was thinking or feeling at that time. I think I just flipped into survival mode and stopped feeling anything. Except exhausted - I felt that. My body remembers. It feels a weariness - a combination of lethargy and tension at the same time. My memories of living on the property are overshadowed by a feeling of utter debilitation. But I pressed through it; I didn't have time to be debilitated.

I spent the days taking care of kids, making food, and washing dishes and clothes in the creek. I tried to cut the grass around the shed with a heavy push mower to keep the snakes and rodents away. The weeds were thick and tall, and it seemed a relentless job to keep the jungle at bay; nevertheless, I tried it a little at a time. Every single thing that needed to be done was a very long process because there were no systems in place. We had no electricity, no running water, no lighting, no easy way to clean things up. It was like living life "from scratch."

Many of my memories revolve around the creek that ran along one side of the property. It was both a life-giver and a threat. It provided water to wash with and bathe, and a cold place to keep our food. But it was also menacing when it rained hard because it turned into a churning river. When we moved there, we had no idea what we were in for with the coming floods.

Our shed was planted next to the creek because the trees that grew next to it "hid us" better than if we were out in the field on the other side of the property (Devlin was all about hiding!). It also made daily living more practical, as most activities revolved around going up and down the bank for water.

The water was cold. Even in the blistering days of summer, it remained cold. It originated from the side of a mountain not far from us. The bottom was a mixture of gravel and sandy places. I dug out the pebbles from a small area of it, to make a "well" that was a few inches deeper than the rest of the creek. Here I carefully positioned a plastic milk crate - the ones that are used by dairy companies to carry gallon jugs of milk to their destinations. This became our "refrigerator." Devlin tied a rope to the milk crate so that it wouldn't float away, and attached the other end of the rope to a concrete cinder block he threw in the middle of the creek. We would put our soy milk in the crate, or air-tight containers of cooked soup or rice. This was important because cooking was difficult. If I could cook once and have *two* meals, it made a big difference. The cold water would flow through the crate and around the containers, keeping them at a decent enough temperature not to spoil.

Washing dishes took a very long time. Because we did not have running water, we had two options - creek water, or spring water. The creek was obviously laden with bacteria, particularly due to the cow pastures upstream, but the spring was about 15 miles from our house and that water had to be hauled in. It was about a 1-1/2 hour ordeal any time I needed to make a trip for water. We had seven 5-gallon buckets and if I adjusted them correctly in the back of the station wagon, I could make five of them fit. The other two buckets got squeezed behind the front seats at my kids' feet.

The spring was large and gushed out from underneath a massive rock, creating an open pool of water which, in turn, traveled through a culvert under the road and became its own "creek" on the other side. The spring was actually considered very pure when tested by the state. You did have to pay attention to where you scooped the water from though. Directly under the rock, where the water flowed fast, was the cleanest.

I would take the buckets and sink them down below the water. Lifting them up was a Herculean effort for me, since each weighed over 40 pounds. Hauling them to the car was so difficult, as they were heavy and clumsy to carry. The thin metal handles dug into my hands. I staggered under the weight, the buckets banging against my legs, causing instant bruises. Hoisting them onto the station wagon platform, and thrusting them into the right spot so they would all fit again, was very demanding. My 90-pound body was not built to lift 40-pound buckets above my waist. Some days I ran out of strength before they were all loaded. When I was halfway done, I would glance at the other 120 pounds still to be carried and wrestled into the car, and I broke down into tears.

Within a few months my female organs felt like they were prolapsing. I had read enough prior in childbirth books to suspect it (by the description of symptoms), but I didn't grasp the potential danger I was in. I was hurting, but had to just "keep on keeping on," pain or no pain. We had to have water. We couldn't survive without it.

There were summers where we experienced drought, and the spring ran low and slowed to a trickle. During that time, creatures vied for the water and obtaining pure water was not easy. We had to scoop it from the bottom of the now-shallow pool where we would see the occasional algae-eater dart away.

On a few occasions when Devlin brought water home, it had tadpoles swimming around in the bucket. When I showed them to him, he said "Ah, just strain them out. It's okay." (Just for the record, I did not! It got dumped after he left) I was not excited about drinking tadpole water!

At home, I would begin unloading the buckets and hauling them up the steps. The buckets were stacked 3 high on the top step, and only one bucket at a time was brought in the shed for use.

I had a little tin cup that I dipped the water out with. It took about 8 dips from the bucket to fill the pot for soup. Twelve dips to fill the dishpan to rinse the dishes. Twelve more dips to fill the dishpan again to wash the dishes with soap. Twelve more dips to rinse the soap off. Because it was such a process to obtain water, I conserved as much as humanly possible. The last rinse water was saved for later to wash the next batch of dishes, or used as "soaking water" for pots that had cooked-on food. I remember when Devlin finally drilled a hole near the bottom of a bucket and attached a small spigot. When I turned the lever and water trickled out, I was so excited! It was as close as we would ever get to "running water."

The temperature of the water depended on the weather. In the summer it was warm and wanted to grow algae. In the winter it was icy-cold and froze my hands. Sometimes the process of heating up water on the wood stove was too time-consuming, so I just washed the dishes as fast as possible, taking breaks every few minutes to warm my hands up next to the stove.

As always though, Devlin had a good reason for all of this. It was our break into self-sufficient living. It would be hard for awhile, he said, but would "pay off" in the end - it would just take a little time. We were off the grid, dependent on nobody, and would soon get systems in place. We could build our little homestead where we could fulfill our dreams. Nothing would be further from the truth.

12

THE LIES WE TELL OURSELVES

I never liked camping. Perhaps it was due to the negative experiences of camping in childhood, where harsh Montana storms destroyed our tents and rainwater leaked into our sleeping bags. I hated the mosquitos that always found their way in and would buzz around my ears. I liked the ramen noodles in a cup we ate by the campfire, and hotdogs and marshmallow roasts, but hated the smoke and waking up cold in the morning. It was never really my thing. And here I was, again. This camping experience, however, wouldn't end for a *very* long time.

I guess by looking at it like camping, it helped stave off the harsh reality that we didn't really have a home. It made living in a shed feel like "a step up" - it was more solid than a tent, after all. Anybody could camp for a few months, right? I wasn't some sensitive flower that would wilt under the slightest inconvenience. I was resilient and tough, and though I was little in size, I was tenacious in spirit. I would make the best of this rough period.

I took our move to the property in stride, hopeful yet

again that the change of scenery and the slow progress towards Devlin's dream would fuel a better relationship between us. Devlin always talked about how relationship bonds were formed by "hard work." This would definitely be hard work. I had no idea *how* hard.

"Southern girls don't sweat - they sparkle."

Yeah, nope. This is definitely sweat.

Wet beads formed on my upper lip, and I wiped them away, agitated.

Who sweats on their upper lip? Ugh! This is ridiculous!

I trudged towards the creek bank with the large white bucket swinging next to me, thumping against my leg with every second step. My irritation surprised me. I considered myself a fairly patient person, but I became unglued in the heat. I actually had "heat and cold intolerance" - a medical symptom - but at the time I just thought I needed to try harder to be patient.

You have nothing to complain about. Yes it's hot, so what? It's summer, it's supposed to be hot. Stop whining.

My body did not agree. The sun's rays were already very intense by midmorning, and I felt dizzy, nauseated, and somewhat stupid.

Mind over matter, mind over matter.

As the bucket sank down in the creek and the water gushed in, I mentally ticked through what I needed to accomplish that morning; fill the tub, nurse the baby, begin the laundry. I slogged back up the bank, the water sloshing out of the bucket, spraying me with droplets. I hated being wet.

Stop complaining. You're already drenched in your own juices.

It's funny, the dialogues we have in our own heads.

I stumbled clumsily across the yard, leaning heavily to one side to help offset the weight of the bucket. When I reached the bathtub, I set it down. Breathless, I paused for a few moments before lifting it back up and dumping the water out. It splattered onto the plastic tub bottom, spraying more droplets my way, as it circled down around the edges, creating small waves.

Up to this point, we had been using a 5-gallon bucket to take baths in. The kids at least were small enough to fit in it, one at a time. They looked oddly like a jack-in-the-box; their bodies almost entirely submerged with little heads poking out. Last week, however, Devlin had gleaned an old tub from a customer who had remodeled her bathroom. He hauled it home and deposited it in the yard next to the house.

"Just pour a couple buckets of water in it in the morning, and by the end of the day it will be warm enough so you can throw the kids all in there together." Those were the instructions.

In one sense, it was a bit better than trying to heat the water up. We had only one small propane gas tank for cooking, and heating up water for baths drained the tank quickly. The downfall however, was that the tub required much more water in order for it to be deep enough to get the kids clean. I needed to take four more trips up and down the bank. There was always a trade off - work harder and save resources, or conserve strength and run out of money, gas, or food. I always chose to work harder.

Living outside in the yard the majority of the time meant the kids were constantly covered in dirt. Mae was attracted to it - like ants to a picnic - and she spent her days sprinkling it in her hair and patting it on her arms. Emma liked to help Mae cover herself with dirt, and the baby was still in the crawling stage, so he was a dustball. They required at least one bath a day, sometimes two baths depending on the circumstances.

I stared at the water in the tub. It was not entirely clean to begin with, as there was always algae from the creek that invariable came along with it. I sighed and turned away. I knew later that evening I would have to fish out several drowned insects or an occasional frog before letting the kids play in it. I couldn't worry about a bit of algae.

Bored with his toys, Micah began fussing. It was his nap time. I quickly made my way down the creek bank again for another bucket of water, wondering if he would hold out just a few more trips. He would not. His cry escalated to a full-blown wail as I stumbled up with the bucket. Filling the rest of the tub would have to wait. I walked over to his blanket I had spread out in the grass and he crawled towards me. I scooped him up.

"Hey Buddy, is it sleepy-time?"

Emma came skipping over.

"Hey, Mom, see my stone!" She shoved a grey piece of gravel in front of my face.

"Lovely."

"I am building a house with rocks!" she crowed, as she bent over to gather more.

I glanced at Mae, who was several feet away, busy sprinkling dirt on a pile of rocks. I laughed.

Emma has a sidekick.

I turned and went inside the shed to nurse the baby.

The shed was hot, but it gave a degree of relief from the sun rays. Holding Micah in one arm, I propped the door open with a shoe. It quickly became stifling inside if there was no air movement. Two flies buzzed in and started a game of tag with each other.

I sat down on the bed and Micah snuggled up to me. I watched the flies whiz around the room, chasing each other. My body was achy. It was only 9 a.m., but the day already felt long.

After the baby was asleep, I grabbed a second bucket to begin the laundry. The girls had moved on from piling rocks and had decided to pick flowers that they could "replant" around their house of stones. They yanked the blossoms of white clover from their stems, and patted them onto the gravel.

I went back down the bank for more water. Laundry was never my favorite task, but living on the property made it absolute misery. A part of me says I shouldn't complain - many people all over the world wash their clothes in a stream. It just wore me out so much and was such a time-consuming ordeal. It took many trips down the slippery creek bank, and then back up to the grassy area, to do the laundry. I suppose if I didn't have tiny children to watch, I could have just stayed at the creek bottom and washed the clothes on the rocks and it would have been a lot more efficient. But it was not safe for them.

The washing-board was something like what you would see in a historic-American museum, or as an interior decorating item in an old-fashioned country store. It was not nostalgic for me, however - it was purely functional. It consisted of a small frame of wood with two "legs" and a rippled metal sheet.

I tossed a few shirts into the bucket of water and added a dribble of liquid detergent. I sunk the washboard into the bucket and swished it back and forth to agitate the clothes. Then I lifted them up, one by one, and scrubbed them against the metal sheet. The water was cold and bubbly. I stared at the bubbles as I swished the clothes again, half mesmerized by their delicate spheres, and halfway in a sleepy stupor from the heat.

Satisfied with that "load" of laundry, I wrung the shirts out and tossed them into a second bucket of water. I went through the same process again to rinse them - all this to clean a few items. Back down the bank I went for another bucket of water. Then another, then another. I did load after load. Laundry for five people was not a simple task, but one item at a time I got it done, stopping every once in a while to check on the baby. After all was said and done, I hung them on a string - my makeshift clothesline - to dry.

The cloth diapers took longer. They would go through three wash and rinse cycles to get the smell out. I had to wash them often because their dampness, combined with the heat, made them a great host for mushrooms. If I left the soiled diapers one day too long, little mushrooms would spring up on the fabric, eating away at it, and I would have to throw them away. I had to be very diligent about this.

With the last piece of clothing hung, I focused on getting lunch ready. Micah woke up and wanted to be held. He always wanted to be held. He was rarely happy playing by himself or with his sisters. He wanted me to be holding him all the time.

Sighing, I took a long piece of fabric and wrapped it around me like a sling, tying a tight knot. I wrangled him into it. It was about as easy as trying to stuff an octopus into a bagpipe, but we managed. I tightened the knot. Doing everything with him on my back took much more energy, but at least it was more peaceful than listening to him whine and cry to be held while I scrambled to get things done.

Our day continued on, one task at a time. Lunch took at least an hour to prepare. Then came wiping down the kids just enough so they could actually eat food without eating the dirt that covered their hands and faces. Then washing dishes. Nursing the baby. Hoeing up some dirt for a garden.

On rare occasions in the summer, I would take the kids down to a shallow bend in the creek and let them splash around in the water, or collect rocks from the bottom to build bridges and dams. Despite my love-hate relationship with the creek, the kids loved it. The banks were covered with tree roots and water plants. Crayfish hid in the muddy areas in hollowed-out holes between the roots. Emma loved to take a stick and poke in the holes, hoping to spot one. If a crayfish darted out, she would run away screaming. Mae tried to catch the dragonflies that flitted from one twig to another. Micah mostly sat in a shallow spot of pebbles and splashed the water with his hands. I was constantly on the lookout for snakes and snapping turtles.

I believed our situation would be temporary. It's what kept my hope alive. As the weeks and months passed by, I never doubted that soon we would make more progress on building the house, and one day move into it, and things would get better. I worked so hard during the day - my contribution to moving things forward. I would go inside the shed at night and lay down, too tired to move - too tired to even close my eyes! I would stare at the ceiling, fixated on the dark nothingness, and wonder how many more days we would live like this.

I would leave the door to the shed open as long as possible at night, to let the cool mountain air come in. Regardless how hot it was during the day, the night always brought cooler air. There was a trade-off: leaving the door open meant the possibility of mice and other creatures coming in. Closing the door meant the heat was trapped in. I never dwelt long on the possibilities of what was out there in the yard or the woods. My mind couldn't handle it. I was unarmed, with babies. Devlin refused to let me have a weapon.

It was good that I was not scared of the dark, because it was *very* dark. There were times I would hear scuffling in the woods and get spooked. I would lay still as a stone, barely moving or breathing. Very slowly I would stretch my foot towards the door, then kick it hard to slam it shut. The rising heat woke me up again in the morning.

13

TODAY I WILL BE NUMB

Green sunlight filtered down through the trees and created patterns of light across the ground. The air was misty from the dew that was already evaporating in the heat of the morning. In a different setting it could have been magical. But I was already dreading today. I did not want this day.

A heavy sadness rose in my chest, like a balloon suddenly inflated, and worked its way up into my throat, as if it were trying to escape my mouth and find freedom in the sky above. I choked it back.

Stinging tears pricked my eyes. I blinked hard, refusing to let them triumph. If a cry escaped, I knew I wouldn't be able to hold back the flood, and I had no time for emotions today. It would be a battle against heat, and I was already behind in the game.

Today I would be numb. Being robotic is how you survive. The world can be hard and callous - its elements unchanging in character despite your deepest agony or pain. The laws of nature are relentless. Gravity, for example, is indifferent - it doesn't care how you feel about it. It will affect you just the same as it does every other creature on the planet. Nature - and people for that matter - can be heartless, merciless; as unsympathetic as a stone.

So we shut down. When we cannot deny a cruel reality, our brain switches gears. Denial is an anesthetic we will willingly guzzle, trying not to miss a drop, if it will temporarily numb our emotions. Perhaps our minds know that the emotional part of our brain is the most delicate and will break first. So it shuts it off, for the sake of preserving our will to survive. The will must endure.

I swallowed the sadness, the fear, and the exhaustion, and began my work for the day. My daily agenda was based on the weather, and in summer that meant doing everything necessary before noon, when it became so hot we had to find cover under the trees, or risk heatstroke. The air in the shed was still and stifling, with no cross-ventilation to draw breezes in. The only thing that room drew in was the flies.

Today I had to begin with watering the plants. Devlin had cleared 2 whole acres of weeds, turning it into a field of dust with his grandiose ideas for a large garden. He had instructed me how to plant the seeds before he had left town, and despite feeling like an ignorant child while he educated me in "the proper way" to put them in the ground, I had succeeded in actually doing it his way - the *right* way, that is.

The seedlings had come up, despite the rock-hard Tennessee soil they had been planted in. This was not his mother's backyard in Romania, despite what he wanted to believe. The dirt here was red, heavy clay, and not conducive to tender sprouts by any stretch of the imagination. The parched ground would swell when watered, making a temporary appearance of fertility, but as soon as the afternoon sun evaporated it, the dirt would again harden and constrict, cracking in some places, and slowly strangle the delicate stems. I had to be careful to not let them wilt and die. But this required an enormous amount of labor.

The garden had been tilled on the side of the property *opposite* the creek. This meant water had to be hauled in large buckets, by hand, all the way across the 5 acres. It was an enormous task. I wasn't prepared for this kind of labor, nor was I strong enough to carry such an outrageously heavy load. But I tried. I tried so hard. I hauled buckets and buckets of water every day, back and forth across the field in the morning and again in the evening, scooping out water with a cup and pouring it around the growing shoots. I *had* to keep them alive.

Despite my best attempts however, many of them shriveled up and died; the work wasted. The environment was too hostile for them. Well, for both them *and* me. Even now my body has never fully recovered from the abuse it suffered during this time.

There were some plants that survived, mainly the cucumbers. Today, I began the descent down the creek bank one more time. The water swirled downstream in slow currents. I plunged the bucket below the surface, creating a vacuum that sucked the water in. Dragonflies zipped and hovered around, curiously watching me. I paused before lifting it back out. I needed just a few more seconds.

Out of the corner of my eye, something darted through the water, black and quick. I peered around the bend and focused intently in the direction it went. Then I saw it, still and motionless below the water. A water snake. A very *large* water snake.

Letting go of the bucket handle ever so slowly, I inched backwards, searching quickly for a stone - any stone large enough to make a difference - while keeping one eye on the threat. My hand grasped the only one of decent size, and I crept alongside the bank, advancing ever so slowly toward the snake. I would only get one shot at this.

Aiming the best I could with feet uneven on the slope, I bent my knees, anticipating my need to run, then quickly hurled the rock at the head of the ugly creature, which was sticking up ever so slightly above the waterline.

My aim was close, but not accurate enough for a fatal blow. The snake sprung out of his nook, and wriggled through the water with Olympic speed. I jumped back, losing my balance, but thankfully catching myself on the knotted weeds that lined the slippery bank. He disappeared into the dark hollow spaces around the bend.

I had missed. Which meant I would have to be on careful lookout from now on. Snakes in and of themselves did not bother me, but I was not familiar with which ones were poisonous and I didn't care to take any chances. The creek felt less safe than ever as I retrieved my bucket and headed back up the bank. A ripple of vulnerability trickled down through my soul, like the water dribbling off my boots. I hated that feeling. It was a reminder that I was indeed in an unsafe world, unprotected, and, for the most part, unable to defend myself from the things that would harm me. Like a hypnotizing snake, the feeling of helplessness is paralyzing.

I set the bucket down, and took a deep breath, willing all feelings away. Though they had punctured through my numbness, they would not win. I had too much to do, and I still needed to hurry.

For the next hour I transported water to the garden, being interrupted a few times by the children who were impatient for breakfast. They did not understand how much harder it would be for me as the day got hotter; they only understood their boredom in the shed.

I finally gave up on the watering and set about making breakfast, getting them dressed, and swatting at flies that accumulated on the counter - and every other surface available. I hated the flies; they were as relentless as the heat.

The day wore on, as I washed pails and pails of laundry and hung it out to dry. By early afternoon I set a blanket out under the trees and placed the kids down on it for a nap. It was time to be still, to keep as cool as possible. I felt guilty stopping my work, and was very much on edge. It was as if Devlin's disapproval had spanned the 400 miles from Savannah to Tennessee, and was now present, reminding me of my laziness and inadequacy. Heat shouldn't stop anybody, he believed; everyone just wants an "easy life full of breaks and vacations." Reality forced me to stop however - it was vital to survive.

The bees were swarming. As I laid down on the blanket, sweat beading up on my forehead and neck, I heard their distinct hum. Devlin owned many hives of honeybees, ranging over the years from 3 to 40 hives. It was a hobby of his which he made me responsible for when he was gone. It was my job to keep a watch on them for swarm activity as the weather got hotter. If he was working locally, I was to alert him immediately so he could prevent them from leaving the hives and flying away, resulting in lost money from honey sales and bees. A hive of bees at that time cost about $100.

Apparently, these bees had decided it was too hot for them as well, and it was time to move on. I watched as they circled up in a black cloud and moved toward the tree line, the air loud with their buzzing. Normally I would prevent them from going, by flinging water at them from a bucket, or starting up the lawnmower. Bees who think rain is coming, or cannot hear the queen (the leader), will settle down in a clump until they reorient themselves or the weather again becomes conducive to flying. There were some days when I couldn't get the mower started, and hauling one more bucket of water was impossible. If that happened, Devlin had instructed me to take the closest metal item I could find - such as a piece of aluminum drainpipe or pot lid, and bang on it with a large stick to make noise so the bees could not hear their leader. I stood there, in the tall weeds, for an hour, banging on metal, like some crazy woman consumed by mental illness. He would then hightail it home from his job and go about his business of collecting the bees back in the hive. On those days, I was the "good" wife, and received attention and affection from him, and promises that our life would get better soon. They were empty promises, of course, but I needed something to hope for. I was wearing out from the days of endless work just to keep everybody fed and alive. I needed something to fan the flame of hope that was slowly dying within me. So I hustled, ever hoping that the more I did, the closer we got to a better future. If nothing else, it would temporarily appease him, as his aggravation with me and the children was slowly increasing every day.

I didn't know how to handle his anger. I felt trapped, unsure what to do when he would go into a rage. It was usually due to the children. He wanted my full attention when he was present - wanted me focused on whatever task at hand he felt I should be doing. I had become the slave, who was not to be distracted by anything else. The children, however, needed attention. Some were not potty trained yet, the baby was in diapers and still nursing. They had basic needs. Like all children, they cried when they were hungry, tired, or frustrated. When their needs interfered with his progress, he was irritated and decided they just needed "discipline." After all, every child between the ages of 0 and 4 years old should be able to sit on a blanket for hours and amuse themselves, without screaming or needing constant interaction.

Yeah, right.

When he would finally lose his temper, he would grab the

first thing available and switch them with it. Sometimes it was his belt, sometimes a plastic clothes hanger. It would take him only 2 seconds to go from "irritated" to full on assault, and I never knew when that would happen. I constantly lived on edge, watching for any signs of impending violence. Violence was his way of showing them who was boss, and wielding power and control. It is stupid to believe that a child should never whine or cry, but he did.

"If you don't get them under perfect control by the time they are three years old, when they are twelve you will have a devil on your hands!" His line of reasoning was always outrageous and stupid. I believed in teaching children self-control and acceptable behavior, but not by beating it into them.

Of course, I would always try to intervene, using my body as a block between him and them. He would always find a way to reach around me and deliver one more blow, simultaneously yelling at me that the reason they were so terribly out of control was because I didn't discipline them as I should. I should have them under perfect control by now. He would storm out of the room, disgusted, but not until he got his final point across by his menacing presence. He would pause, as if potentially plotting another assault, and make comments about my mothering and lack of wisdom. This was the moment where I never knew what would happen next. He would either leave with a sneer and nasty comment, or would re-focus his attention on another "disobedient" toddler. These were the only times I fought with him and questioned out loud his behavior. I subconsciously knew that my children's survival depended on my survival, so I would normally stay quiet when he was irate. In the middle of these fights though, I would protect them at any cost.

Afterwards, I would be the one to hold and comfort the beaten child, then developing bruises, while determining how to keep the other two safe. Sometimes Devlin would decide the next activity to "get things in order around here," and demand that they follow him to do something useful. That meant being on higher alert, to avoid a second explosion.

During his violent outbreaks, I hated him. Pure, unbridled hatred rose up in my gut and filled my body with rage. I started shaking with the fury, as adrenaline again surged through my veins. The mother bear in me awakened and she was absolutely and vehemently *furious*. Had it not been for his greater strength, I would have attacked him, relentlessly and without mercy. Hurting my children, bruising their bodies, and terrifying their minds, unleashed in me an anger that I could barely contain.

But knowing his power, I stayed in check. It was safer for them if I protected them in another way - by mitigating all the circumstances that would lead up to another attack from him. I became an expert at walking on eggshells and trying to do everything in my power to prevent his angry outbursts. I controlled every single variable I could.

Growing up in abuse, I was used to this behavior. It had been normalized, even though it was in no way safe. I had been taught that if I could just be good, and keep the kids good, it would be okay. That deception would keep me trapped for 7 more years.

Thankfully, it would not always be this way. Though we suffered for years under his brutality, I would one day become stronger than he was. As menacing as he was, he had a break in his armor, and that was his foolish pride. It would eventually cause him to make mistakes that enabled us to break free. My day was coming.

14

HOPE OF A SUNFLOWER

The next time Devlin came home, it was just long enough to put a tar-paper roof onto the third shed. I mean, the *utility building* (which it was legally classified as, years later).

The "utility building" was much larger than the two smaller sheds - the base floor was 40 x 16 feet. He wanted to make it big enough for his beekeeping hobby later, but decided that he would finish off one room at a time, until the whole thing was livable. He never made it past the first room however, which was 12 feet by 16 feet, so it was still the size of a shed as far as living space went. We lived in that one room for the next few years. He filled the other remaining space up with random junk he hoarded. It would become the storage room for broken appliances, broken tools, building materials, bee equipment, rolls of insulation, gardening buckets, rusted furniture, vehicle parts, and who knows what else.

In the one room where we would live, a full-sized mattress took up a majority of one wall, with space left for the door to swing in. Devlin would eventually move an industrial-sized sink in that would take up the majority of another wall. Between the wood stove and recycled cabinets that he brought from yet another customer's remodeled house, we ended up with another very small space to live.

Still, it was an "upgrade" from the tiny shed, and so it felt like an improvement. My spark was slowly being snuffed out. Little things like more living space - even if it was only a few feet - was enough to keep my hope alive.

It is hard to describe life in the shed, as the days went by in a haze of exhaustion. I did much more than just wash dishes and clothes and babies, cook food, and try to keep a dying garden alive. Yet it is hard now to remember exactly how the days passed by - they were so long and weary. Most of the time was spent just doing the daily things necessary to survive.

The weeks would turn into months and seasons. Summers would turn into falls, which turned into cold, hard winters. Devlin came and went depending on his whims. He usually only stayed a few days at a time, mostly working out of state. Once in a while he would get a local job, and then he would be around for a few weeks before disappearing again. The majority of the time I was left to survive solo.

Our methods of surviving changed by the season. I was constantly adapting things to preserve strength, energy, and money. In the summers, when I became so weary from the heat exhaustion and could not haul one more bucket of water from the creek, I took advantage of the afternoon rain. When heavier rains would come, I would give the kids a bar of soap to play with and sent them to run around in the grass in their underwear to take a "shower." Afterwards they would come in sopping wet, but relatively cleaner than before.

Some "improvements" to our living situation failed. The second year we lived there, Devlin got a great idea to create a "shower." He took another used bathtub he had gleaned from somewhere and put it in the storage area. He then used the 1000-gallon honey holding tank he had purchased for his beekeeping hobby as a water-holding tank which he dragged to the side of the shed. He attached a pipe that went from the tank, through a hole in the side of the storage room, and to the tub. Now, a trickle of water could be turned on and off with a small lever. He filled the tank up with creek water using a sump pump and pronounced it a success.

"Success" was a bit too enthusiastic. It was *gross*. The water smelled horrible and was very slimy. The tank was too high up for me to see into, but it did not have a lid, and I imagine many bugs, and perhaps birds and other animals might have fallen into it and got trapped and died, making a soup of decaying tissues. After two showers, I refused to use it again. We would bathe in the creek with the snakes first!

In the winter our method changed again. Baths took place inside the shed in a small storage tote. I would fill it up with a few inches of water and cycle kids through the same water, adding a little more hot water for each kid, as it cooled off very fast. Later on, when Devlin would move a sink inside the shed, we would use that instead.

Summers were spent trying to stay cool and winters trying to stay warm. I gathered fresh peppermint leaves and red clover and lemon balm in the summer to make cold drinks to cool the children off, and in the winter I made tea on the wood stove to efficiently warm everyone up from the inside out. I tried to utilize any information I had and make it work for me.

Unfortunately, my energy was also spent on many distractions that Devlin called "projects." Before he would leave to work out of state again, he would invent some project that "needed to be taken care of," and dump the responsibility on me. They were always ridiculous things - time-consuming and not worth fooling with - but he told me it was my way of "contributing" to us getting ahead. Once he came home with about 20 used vehicle headlights. They were covered in grime and filth. He had gotten them at a junkyard for a few dollars and my job was to clean them up and then list them on Ebay to sell to make money. He thought this would be an "easy way" to make a few extra dollars. This meant me cleaning them with a toothbrush in a creek (and of course not getting any water in the electrical parts) while watching three toddlers in the sweltering heat. Then I needed to dry them, take photos with a half-broken camera, then make a trip to the library in town and upload the photos online and create selling descriptions. I also was supposed to spend time researching which vehicles a headlight was compatible with, to improve the listings and chance of selling them.

In the winter, projects included things like taking care of his hobbies - feeding the bees. Every day it would take me an hour or two to gather the mason jars off of 40 beehives, fill each one up with sugar syrup, and reposition them on the hives, while trying not to smash curious bees at the opening, or get stung. The bees were always aggressive and came after me. The bulky bee suit I clomped around in smelled like bad cheese (due to a chemical used in beekeeping) and had holes in it which the bees would always find. Making the sugar syrup meant stirring hard clumps of sugar (laced with mouse droppings and chewed up bits of the sugar bags) into buckets of ice-cold water with a large tree branch, hoping it would dissolve. It took so much time. It seemed Devlin just invented projects to keep me busy.

I tried so hard to help us get ahead. Not only did I take care of Devlin's projects, but I also did things to try to offset our expenses so we would have more money to "build the house." The first summer while Devlin was gone, I drove one morning to a flea market an hour away to sell produce from our garden for money. At that time, we had no money left. I had to judge how far the flea market was, to make sure I could make it on the gas I had left in the car, with hope I would make enough money at the market to buy gas to get home.

I woke up at 4 am to get ready. The night air was still cool, and I needed to work fast because when the sun came up, it brought the scorching heat. With the headlamp fastened to my forehead, and a bucket in each hand, I headed across the dark field to the green bean bushes.

I had spent every morning that summer picking disgusting, squishy, yellow bean bug larvae off of those plants, one by one. It had finally paid off and our green bean plants were extremely prolific. In an hour and a half I picked ten gallons of large, flat green bean pods. Next, I moved to the cucumber patch and gathered as many as I could. This was the only produce that was ready to harvest. It would have to do.

Walking back to the shed, I entered the storage room and lifted two boxes of jarred honey off the floor. They had already been sealed and labeled a while ago. This is what would bring in the most money. I set them down in the back of the station wagon. It was 6 a.m. I would have to leave soon.

I gathered whatever food I could find to feed the children later, and put it in a bag. Then I collected some diapers and clothes for them into another bag. I lifted each child from the bed and placed them in their car seats. I prayed they would sleep as long as possible. It was so hard to be responsible for everything myself. I was hoping to catch just enough of a break to get things somewhat set up at the market before all of three of them were demanding things from me.

The car started, and I was relieved. The gravel popped and crackled beneath the tires as I started down the driveway. I glanced across the field at the sunflowers that had bloomed.

They had been sown from a package of leftover seeds from years past. Devlin had slung the seeds out to get rid of them, but they had taken root and produced beautiful blossoms that reached toward the sunshine. I stopped the car.

Grabbing a pair of scissors that I had snatched on my way out the door that morning ("just in case"), I crossed the field and cut down ten of the prettiest bright yellow sunflowers, leaving them with long stems. Their prickly stems stabbed my fingers as I gathered them into a bucket filled with creek water, and plopped them down on the passenger seat. I would sell them for $1 at the flea market, as "fresh flowers." Mostly they just drew attention to our table.

I worked very hard that day, balancing the needs of three restless children behind a tiny wooden table, while talking and selling to customers. My mind was in constant motion, being drawn in all directions, without stopping. I was glad when the afternoon came and the market slowed to a crawl. I had sold $80 worth of beans, cukes, and honey. I was so proud.

On the way home I was able to buy gas *and* stop at the store for some necessary food for the week, with $30 left over. I had been resourceful and used what I had at my disposal and multiplied it. It felt like a good day.

The ride home was difficult as I could barely stay awake, but I was pleased. It had been so long since I had a felt a moment of delight or elation, and I clung to that speck of happiness as long as I could, even if it only existed in some half-wilted but vibrant little sunflowers, rocking back and forth in the seat next to me. It would be years before I would feel another moment of lightheartedness; perhaps this is why this memory stands out above the rest. It was the light amid the ever-darkening sunset of events that would affect our lives in deep and painful ways.

The winters would come. There would be harder days

where we strove to just keep warm, and fight for survival when we got sick. There would be days where I almost gave up hope that anything would get better and the nights where I prayed that God would not to let me wake up to another morning. But this day...on this day the hope was enough. And I smiled.

15

THE FLOODS

The rain pelted against the metal roof. It had never been a sound I particularly liked - I always found it annoying, not peaceful. But now... now every time I heard it, a tight knot formed in the pit of my stomach.

I am angry. So angry.

In my mind I visualize myself screaming irately, yet desperately, at my younger self.

"What is wrong with you? Get out! Leave! You don't have to stay here! He doesn't control you. Look at you, you're going to die like this!"

But she couldn't hear me. She didn't know there were other options. And, truth be told, at that time, he did control her. The strongest bonds are not chains or bars. They are the lies we believe. The false perceptions we hold as truth. Those are our true chains.

The rain got louder and came down harder. The air felt humid and very heavy. Time started counting down. I pulled on my mud boots and coat and tossed some toys onto the mattress for the kids.

"I'll be right back."

I went outside and trudged over to the creek bank. The water was rising. The currents moved rapidly, much faster than normal. That was all I needed to know. I had about one hour.

I clomped back to the shed and up the steps, poking my head through the door.

"Mom needs to do some stuff outside. I'll be back in a little bit." They were playing with plastic toy dishes.

"Ok! I am cooking eggplant!" Emma announced as she pretended to slice a plastic vegetable.

"Great," I replied, and disappeared out the door.

I had to move fast. I scanned the woodline where the creek was rushing. Everything had to go. I grabbed the wheelbarrow and started piling things into it. Anything remotely close to the water would be washed away if it was not moved now. I felt my stomach grow tight. There was *so much* stuff, so many random things! How would I ever do this?

I grabbed the laundry buckets. Devlin's construction tools. The toolboxes. I spied garden shovels and car parts I knew he just bought. They all needed to be moved to higher ground, which meant on the other side of the 5 acres. The field never looked so big. I pulled the kids tricycles and doll buggy across the field, hoping that the water wouldn't reach them there. All of the seedlings that had sprouted in their plastic cups got moved up on the shed steps to go inside.

I carried the buckets of spring water that we had for drinking, one by one, up the stairs of the shed, and swung them through the door, with a "thud!" onto the floor.

The quiet trickling of the creek in winter had turned into a roar of white rushing water. It was not far from spilling out of the bank. The generator had to be moved higher before it flooded. It was our only source of electricity. When it worked, anyway.

It was so heavy. I carefully grasped its cold metal bar and lifted. It barely moved. I searched around and found two scrap 2 x 4 boards and positioned them like ramps against the back of a trailer. I climbed up onto the trailer, lifting the generator again, trying hard to pull the 150-pound beast upward. In spite of its wheels to make it easier to move, it weighed much more than I did, and I stumbled.

The wood jarred and toppled to the ground, causing the generator to tip.

No!

I forced my body against it, trying to steady it, and attempted to balance the remaining wheel on the wood, as I carefully backed it down the ramp. I positioned the wood again, and slowly, slowly dragged the machine up. It took four tries. My legs ached. My abdomen ached. My arms and lungs ached. My face and coat were soaking wet. Water seeped through my skirt and leggings and chilled my legs.

It was not the rain that caused the biggest flood threat. It was flash flooding from the mountain. The valley we lived in got the overflow, not only from the surrounding hills and pastures, but also whatever spilled off the mountain. We were within walking distance to the base of the mountain range. We got it *all*.

The creek bank had begun to overflow and water streamed across the gravel driveway. It sloshed down into the hole where the sewage bucket got dumped. Soon that would overflow. I looked away, ignoring what that meant.

The rooster!

I raced to the chicken coop near the tree line, which was just a round fence of chicken wire with a tarp covering it. I carefully pulled aside the wire and ducked inside. The rooster was panicked and raced around the pen.

"Come on, dummy, I'm trying to save you! Come here…"

He fluttered and flapped, narrowly escaping my efforts to grab him.

"You want to die today? Is that your plan?!"

I had no patience. The water was surging, and I was out of time. The muddy water was two inches deep in his pen. It took another five minutes before I was successful in catching him. Five minutes of time meant a few more inches of water to stand in; it was flooding that fast. The chicken splashed about in the water, not understanding why his usually dusty pen had become a chicken-sized swimming pool.

I was out of breath. I grasped him tightly and climbed out of the chicken wire. It caught my coat and snagged it. As I tried to pull free, clutching the chicken with both arms, the loose wires tore a small hole in my coat and the down feathers fluttered out in the wind. The water came almost halfway up my boots in the deeper sections of the yard. It flooded the road, the grass - everything. I slogged through a lake which minutes before did not exist. The water traveled fast, pushing against my legs. I had no idea it could be that strong. I waded, carefully calculating each step so that I didn't slip. It was hard to keep standing in the currents. The rushing water was all I heard. The rain continued to beat down. I slowly inched my way back to the stairs of the shed. One step had disappeared under the flood. I climbed up, inside, and slammed the door.

"Mama, why did you bring the chicken in?"

I panted. Anxiety swelled in my chest, though the immediate danger should have *seemed* to be over. Water dripped to the floor creating many small puddles.

"The creek..." I gasped.

I don't have energy to explain.

I ignored her, and headed towards the junk room where I found the wire cage we had kept rabbits and chickens in in the past. I deposited the rooster, wet and cranky looking, into it and secured the door spring so he couldn't escape.

I glanced out the window at the rushing water.

God, please make it stop. I can't get out with the kids.

The shed was completely surrounded by water.

Between feeding the wood stove and taking care of the kids and food, I spent the rest of the day watching the stairs. The water creeped up, until it covered the second step. We were in the center of a vast expanse of water - a tiny ark in the middle of an ocean. The water flowed under and around the shed, making me wonder how strong of a flow had to exist before the shed would be dislodged. It was not so much the water itself that scared me, it was the power it had. The currents were strong and I was no match for them myself, much less carrying children. And where would I carry them *to*? We were in the middle of nowhere. It was cold outside, and they were tiny. There was nowhere safe, dry, or warm to run to.

The car would not start in the rain. Water always got in somehow and caused an electrical glitch. Even if I did make it to a remote neighbor, I knew what would come next. Devlin would eventually show up, and make me out to be crazy. He would say I exaggerated the situation, and say that "It was just a little bit of water, it's no big deal. Nobody is going to melt!" And then he would laugh as if everything was okay, and his wife was just being her typical neurotic self. He would covertly shame me in front of them, assure them everything was really fine, and then unleash his anger when he got me back to the shed. My subconscious mind decided it was safer to stay put.

As night settled on the wood line, I strained my eyes to see if it was climbing. Thankfully it seem to crest about halfway through the third stair, and hold steady there. I lit the lantern and hung it on the nail by the door. The dim light shed its rays on the moving water and I watched expectantly, praying fervently that it would stop.

The rain let up and pattered lightly on the roof. The children had fallen asleep. I laid down on the bed, and tried to relax my body which was tense with nervous energy. Tried to calm my racing thoughts. The only sound I could hear was the surging waters.

I was a resilient person. I was resourceful. I had survived brutal days of heat exhaustion, no food, muscle breakdown from overworking, outdoor labor in freezing temperatures until my fingers were so stiff they wouldn't bend. I had given birth to three babies in the bathtub, unassisted, and without pain medications. I had survived physical, emotional, and other abuses unflinchingly.

But now… now I stayed because of fear. Fear that I wouldn't be able to "make it on my own." Fear of his threats. Fear of abandonment with no resources.

How do you keep your children safe and fed if you have nothing to protect them with and nothing to give them? Where do you go when you are not aware that help exists?

I am angry. It could have been prevented. We didn't need to live like this. I didn't need to live with constant fear and exhaustion.

There is a reason I hate the sound of rain.

What keeps someone locked in a situation that is horrible, when they have options to change it? Why do people feel "stuck" when in reality they choices? How is it I lived in sheds for years, barely holding onto life, when there were probably other options available to me? I have come to believe it is because people don't see the options they have, as real options.

My trauma counselor helped bring this to my attention years later. She assured me, "You did the best you could with the resources you had." Yet she tried to get me to think about what my thought processes were at the time. What would my life have looked like if I had left that situation? What if I had just said "I've had enough of this," and had loaded my kids into the car and drove to my sister's house, or a friend's house, and asked for help or a place to stay? My response surprised both of us, I think.

"It never even occurred to me to leave."

"Not once?"

"No."

Something that confuses, and often annoys, people who have not lived dominated by abuse, is the question of why the victim does not leave the abuser.

"Why does she stay with him?"

"If any man hit me, that would be the last time he ever saw me!"

"I wouldn't tolerate mistreatment!"

"I'd get out the first time he ever even thought about mistreating me!"

What they don't understand is that the victim does not see leaving as a viable - or safe - choice. The very option that might gain her freedom and relief, often does not seem like an option at all.

16

RATS IN THE MORNING

I heard their scuffling. Their dirty, little clawed feet scrambled across the floor upstairs and kept me awake at night. I heard them gnawing. Then all would go silent. Minutes later, they would be back, scuffling more. Sometimes I would tell myself they were squirrels. Squirrels are cuter than rats and it's easier to pretend they are nicer.

I tried to ignore them. I had tried before, in vain, to catch them, but it felt pointless - there was no way to keep them out. The roof was unfinished, and they would climb the outside wall - like squirrels - and slither through the open places around the rafters.

I squeezed my eyes shut and pulled the blanket over my face. Winter had come. It was too cold to fall back asleep. The fire in the stove had been out for a while, though I had already been up twice in the night to restart it. The wood stove was small and only held a single log. It would usually burn for two hours before dying out, and it took another hour before the room got so cold it forced me awake.

Cold, rats, or nursing the baby. If it wasn't one thing, it was another. My body felt heavy. Sleep deprivation had taken its toll over the passing months.

It seemed the cold surrounded me from every side. It didn't help that the mattress was lying on an uninsulated floor. At least the girls shared a bunk - if it could be called a bunk. It was basically a rough frame Devlin had fashioned out of 2 x 4's and attached to the wall with two angle supports. There were a few boards nailed on the side which served as rungs to climb up. Warm air rises and it was to their advantage.

The alarm clock went off and I scrambled to silence it. The baby shifted in the bed but did not wake up.

Thank you, God.

It was 4:30 a.m. I felt around in the dark for the headlamp. It hung on a nail above my head at the base of the bunk bed above me. I turned it on. The batteries were dying so the light was dim, and it flickered. I pulled it onto my forehead and adjusted the elastic band around my head.

I crawled carefully around Devlin and off the bed and pulled a faded denim skirt on over my pajamas. I couldn't care less what I looked like - it was dark and I was exhausted; but the skirt - an icon of submission and "modesty" - must be worn.

I checked the children. The baby was still covered. I couldn't see the girls, so I stepped up onto the second board which allowed me to peek over the side rail of the bunk and identify two blanketed bumps. I stretched as far as I could reach over the rail to cover them with another blanket.

I climbed back down and sat on the side of the bed and reached for my mud boots. They were three sizes too big, but the floor consisted only of plywood sub-flooring and stayed absolutely filthy with dirt and mud, despite my best efforts of sweeping it several times a day. Socks would be ruined in minutes. There was really no way to keep the dirt from coming in either; we lived outside half of the time.

The shed door creaked loudly as I opened it and stepped out into the even colder night air. It was foggy and wet outside. The pile of wood, which was hidden under a plastic tarp, was quickly getting smaller. I hoped it would last long enough. I chose several logs to bring back inside. I stacked them together, then lifted the bundle and clumsily hauled them up the steps and into the shed. I clumped across the floor with my heavy boots, trying not to wake the kids. Devlin was still asleep too. I was glad; I didn't have to be on high alert.

I laid the wood on the floor next to the woodstove and carefully opened its metal door. I scooped out whatever ashes I could with a large metal serving spoon and tossed some twigs inside. Over the years I became a pro at lighting the fire. Devlin had showed me how to drizzle a little bit of diesel fuel on the twigs for instant flame. It was not dangerous like gasoline, but it did the trick. I flicked the lighter and the flames were instant. I slowly fed the fire with bigger sticks, letting each catch. Throwing too many on at a time would suffocate it out.

The warmth was so welcome. The little orange flames flickered around the wood, slowly growing into an animated blaze. I spent every night watching them through blurry eyes, mentally urging each twig to catch and burn, so I could return to sleep. When it was burning decently, I added a log and closed the door. I adjusted the draft door of the stove and wiped my ash-covered hands on my skirt.

Next was lighting the kerosene lamp. I hated that lamp. I am sensitive to smells and chemicals and the oil smelled terrible. The off-gassing fumes from the lamp could include dangerous carbon monoxide, so it had to be hung outside the shed door, rather than left to burn inside. It made for very poor lighting, but was a bit better than only having the headlamp. I grabbed a lighter, lit the wick and adjusted it, then hung it on its nail outside. The light came through the dirty glass, subdued, but enough to see by.

Talk about feeling like you are back in time.

It makes me angry to realize that it only took three days after I left the property before Devlin got the electricity company to come out and assess the property to have a temporary electrical pole put in. Three days! If Devlin was to live there, he refused to be inconvenienced, but the children and I lived without electricity for 2-1/2 years.

"Mennonites do it all the time." That was his line of reasoning. It wasn't true, as Mennonites did *not* live the way we did; they had systems in place, and community support - neither which I had. But I had stopped arguing with Devlin a long time ago.

The first winter Devlin was gone, working in Savannah, and would return every few weeks to check in on things, stir up problems, or fiddle with projects. He would only come back for a few days before disappearing again. For the next few days my daily routine would change to adapt to his needs while he was home.

It took an hour and a half to cook breakfast and make Devlin's lunch. Having only one stove burner made everything difficult and time-consuming. It took 50 minutes to make the oatmeal – thirty of that was spent just trying to heat the almost-frozen water up. When the oatmeal started to stick, I carefully scraped it into another container before it burned, washed the pot, and filled it with more water to cook the potatoes, which would take another 40 minutes.

In the meantime, I went out to the storage room to gather

the baskets of laundry and sort them to be washed later that morning. The headlamp was so dim I could barely see. In the winter I took the dirty clothes to the laundromat because it was too cold to do the laundry outside; the creek water was barely above freezing. Devlin refused to cooperate with putting his clothes in a single basket; whichever was closest was where he dropped them. They were covered in grease, drywall chalk, and caulking. It made all of our clothes feel dusty and stiff, even after washing them. I tried to separate his into their own load, even though it meant spending more money at the laundry mat.

When the potatoes were halfway done, Devlin's alarm went off. I scrambled to wash the containers from his lunch from the day before and filled one up with oatmeal. I added the honey, flax seeds, and raisins which were his norm, and sliced an apple and tucked the pieces into the side of the bowl. He never took the time to eat at home, he always ate on the road on his drive to work, so as not to miss a single minute. Such is the life of a workaholic. Or an adulterer. Or a mafia member... whichever he was. I had to package everything up quickly and get it road-ready.

Devlin pulled on his jeans and coat and went outside to visit the outhouse. He did his usual morning routine fiddling with his work van, loading the tools he needed for the day, or hooking up the trailer to haul materials to the job site.

The baby woke up and started crying. I let him cry for a few minutes while I transferred the pot of potatoes to the table, then picked him up and held him on one hip while spooning them into a lunch container. He was still tired and his only interest was in nursing. He head-butted me while I tried to fit a lid on the container, wrapped up some bread and tomatoes, and put everything into a plastic grocery bag - the make-shift lunch box.

I placed the baby on the bed and he cried louder while I

pulled off the heavy mud boots and crawled up on the mattress to nurse him. The fire was dying out. I gathered a blanket around us and tried to ignore the chill in the air.

Devlin came back inside bringing with him a large whoosh of cold air. He spied his lunch and picked it up along with his cell phone. He left without saying a word.

It was probably better that way. He had been so irritable lately that no words were better than angry ones. The diesel engine roared to life and he rumbled away down the gravel road. I breathed a sigh of relief and sadness. The sun was barely beginning to light the sky.

The plan for the day was grocery shopping and laundry; it would take all day. Going to the laundromat was quite an ordeal. And while the goal was small – get the clothes washed - it was never simple. Laundry day meant a lot of hauling, especially on a rainy day like today - I would expend enormous amounts of energy. It meant hauling loads of laundry to the car, carefully navigating the mud puddles, hauling each wiggly child piggyback-style to the car so they wouldn't be covered in mud, hauling the laundry into the laundromat when we reached town, and then hauling the heavy, wet clothes in baskets back to the car. Drying them at the laundromat cost too much money. When we got home, I would again haul the kids and all the wet clothes back inside the shed, and the begin the process of hanging up the laundry around the room. Shirts went on hangers on the rail of the bunk bed or the cabinet handles. Underwear and socks got poked through the thin bars on the wire shelving in a colorful line-up. Pants were hung closest to the fire, and got rotated every few hours.

I spent the next hour getting three kids ready to go into

town and dressed in "acceptable clothes" so we wouldn't look homeless, and then trying to keep them on the bed so they wouldn't be covered in filth from the floor before we even left the property. It took extra time to dress them in double layers because it was so cold. The car had no heating and they would need to endure the cold for quite some time.

We headed out. Or rather we *tried* to - the car would not start. That was nothing new. To say it had "issues" would have been an understatement. It was a new issue every day. While Devlin had originally baited me with a nice vehicle that had no problems, he had eventually downgraded me to something that was broken and completely unreliable. The Mercedes was crumbling on the inside and out. When it rained, water would pour in around the doors and windows, as the seals were cracked and disintegrating. The carpets were spotted with mold because of this inflow, but there was nothing I could do to stop it. Two of the windows were held up with clothespins that Devlin had strategically driven down in between the glass panel and door. The bigger problem, however, was that water leaked into the electrical system and wreaked havoc. A side effect of this was that the radio would turn itself on and off at random and drain the battery. We were often left stuck, and unable to jump start it.

There was also the problem with the starter. Devlin said he knew what the problem was, but didn't want to waste time taking it apart to get to the problem. So he rigged the system, threading two electrical wires to the inside of the car through the air vent. To start the car, I would turn the key, then connect these two wires together until they sparked, and the car would roar to life. Well, sometimes.

Driving anywhere during the summer was dangerous. There was no air conditioning and only one window rolled down. The inside temperature of the car would get close to 120 degrees. We had to open all the doors to let the heat escape for several minutes before getting in and then quickly drive to our next location before we developed "heat headaches." The winter was no better though. The lack of heating caused us to freeze for long periods of time and get sick.

Driving in the rain was also not an option as the windshield wiper mechanism was broken. The shocks were also broken and the rotors unturned, making braking dangerous, and driving down the mountain impossible. I propped the hatchback open with a piece of pipe or a stick when loading or unloading groceries, water buckets, or laundry, because the connecting hinges were broken. Many times the stick would get jarred and the heavy door would fall on me, badly injuring my back or shoulder. The pain was breathtaking.

There were other issues too; I was stranded on the side of the road more times than I can count. Sometimes the engine would just stop in the middle of driving, or at a stoplight. Trying to get several children out of the car and off to the side of the highway was so difficult. Changing a tire was also impossible, because even though I possessed the knowledge to do it, the spare tire was kept in a place that required a lift. The lift was broken and it prevented me from having enough strength to get it out. We were constantly at the mercy of the weather, road hazards, or the finicky electrical system of a car that was notorious for leaving us stranded. Yet, I "had access to a vehicle" and a Mercedes at that! What should I complain about?

Laundry and groceries would not be happening today. We were stuck, again. I looked at the food supply and counted up how many meals I could still pull together - not very many. I hoped Devlin would see the necessity of self-diagnosing the car by tomorrow. He was planning on leaving the state again and if we had no car, it meant we would have no food or water either.

The winter days passed slowly, creeping by like a half-paralyzed slug. Staying warm took a lot of energy. It took up to four hours a day to chop the wood, stack it, and haul it inside. Then I would bring it in, a bundle at a time, to dry out around the fire. Feeding the fire happened every hour, and twice a day I would clean all the ashes out of the tiny stove or it could not get a good draft. My hands felt like sandpaper, roughed up from the splinters and bark. I didn't own gloves; money was tight and buying things for myself felt like a "waste of money." I was tough - a few abrasions or split knuckles were "nothing."

I should just be glad we have a way to stay warm, after all.

I didn't realize how I rationalized everything. Devlin's persistent comments to me over the years had paid off big time for him. His thoughts had gotten into my head and had become my own. His words repeated themselves in my head anytime harsh realities and pain tried to bring me to my senses; I thought his thoughts. His brainwashing had succeeded. I was his pawn and would do whatever he said without question. I had become a captive.

17

WHEN YOUR SOUL IS TIRED

I didn't move. I just lay there, stunned. The shock from the impact stopped me entirely. I was in that three-second pause - the one that happens right before you burst into tears or scream into the air. I ended up doing both. I am not sure how long I did it, but between crying from pain and sheer exhaustion and screaming angry rants about how stupid *everything* in the world was, I found a way to drag myself up the creek bank.

The mud was slick and relentless. I carefully gauged where to put my foot next so as not to slip again. I stumbled, one step at a time, willing myself to get to the top. My hands, skirt, and coat were wet and covered in cold mud. My feet felt frozen in my rubber boots, as the fall down the bank had landed them in the icy-cold water. I felt a sharp pain in my hip and my knees hurt badly. My entire body felt jolted and painful from the impact.

Somehow I made it up the bank and to the shed, dragging the 5-gallon bucket of creek water up the wooden plank steps and through the door. Inside was not comforting, but at least it was warm. I reached for the stool and sat down. I peeled my coat off and then sat with my head between my knees, trying to breathe and gather strength to clean myself off and get about the actual task at hand: heating up the water I had just hauled from the creek.

It took several minutes before I stood up and moved to the huge pot that sat on top of the wood stove. I looped my fingers through the metal handle and lifted the lid, burning them, yet hardly feeling it. My hands were too cold to feel the full effect. When the water in the pot was low, it became very hot. I didn't have a convenient container to mix the cold and hot water together to make it warm, and even if I had it was just one more step. And I was too tired to do one more step. I scooped some water out of the pot with a tin cup, and poured it onto a rag on the rickety wooden table. It lay there limply, steaming for a minute while I waited for it to cool down.

The kids swung on the wooden boards of the bunk above them and asked random questions which I only half heard. I took the rag and cleaned the mud off my hands, and then my clothes, the best I could. Then I took a plastic pitcher and started filling up the pot with the cold creek water. In about an hour it would be warm enough to wash the children. If I could get more wood in the stove to keep the fire going…

I wrestled another log of wood into the stove, throwing some diesel on it. I hoped it would help keep the flames going and keep the heat up until it caught fire. I slammed the door shut and the instant waft of air blew the ashes out in a white and grey cloud of confetti that eventually settled on the floor. In an hour there would be more where that came from, so I ignored it, and began pulling things out from under the industrial sink. It was time to clean off the mold.

The mold on the wall was black and spotty, and had a distinct odor I found awful. Despite scrubbing it off regularly, it would return with a vengeance. It favored the wall connected to the rest of the building because there was no insulation there. The wall would sweat with condensation because of the temperature difference that existed between the outside and inside our room. It was not, however, confined to that wall - that would have been too easy. Nope, the mold threw its little spores everywhere, and it seemed there was not a place anywhere in the room where it didn't pop up in new colonies. It loved the blinds that covered the glass on the front door (it had condensation there to thrive as well). It embedded in the blankets and clothing if I didn't air them out or wash them often enough.

Then there was the green mold that feasted on the wooden cabinet doors and inside the cupboard where I kept the dishes. I tried every way to get rid of it. Mold deterrents, natural remedies, bleach. It always came back. We slept with it, ate with it, and breathed it continually. It was determined - like a ruthless stalker who refused to leave us in peace.

I scrubbed. I scoured. I washed. I rinsed and dried. I wiped it with tea tree essential oil this time - it was too cold outside for me to use bleach - we couldn't ventilate the room. It only took about an hour this time.

Dinner was next on the list, but the kids were getting restless. Being cooped up with only a 5 x 5 foot area of walking space all winter was making them stir crazy. They started running from one side of the room to the other, then flinging themselves onto the bed, shrieking. Thank God they were little - the room probably seemed bigger to them than it really was. Their racing around, however, made it feel like the walls were closing in on me.

The baby howled. He wanted to get off the bed with the other kids, but he couldn't. The floor was too rough and filthy and cold for him to crawl on. He would scrape his little hands and tear up his clothes, and it was freezing.

Nope, they needed to go outside, or it would be a really hard night. I checked where the sun was at - we had about an hour of light left. I bundled them into two layers of clothes, hats, and coats, and took them out into the frigid air. Emma grabbed her doll buggy and asked if I would put the baby in it. I agreed - he needed somewhere safe. She pushed him across the gravel driveway, plastic wheels rattling as they clattered toward the dirt and grass. She loved whizzing him around. Mae instantly found a dirt pile to play in and sprinkle around.

I glanced wearily at the wood pile and decided I better make the best use of time by gathering sticks for fire-starters. The wind had picked up earlier that day, and the ground was littered with broken tree branches and twigs. They had been dead for awhile, just waiting for a strong gust to break them loose. It was like manna falling from heaven to me, because I was so weary of chopping wood. These were practically ready-made for the fire - they just needed collecting. I returned to the shed and went in the back building and grabbed some empty cardboard boxes. The wind was still icy cold. One by one I gathered the wood, snapping the larger ones in half. I wanted to get them inside before it rained. Otherwise it could take days to dry them out. For the next 30 minutes I collected them as fast as I could.

The sun began to sink lower on the horizon, and the temperature dropped. The baby started wailing, tired of being jostled in the doll buggy. I picked him up and coaxed Mae out of the dirt.

"But, Mom, I *love* dirt!"

More wailing, this time from her. At least Emma was halfway compliant. They continued crying and complaining while I hauled the 4 boxes of sticks into the storage room, and stacked them, in a tottering tower, against the wall.

Next came baths for the kids - one at a time, in the sink. Thankfully they were still small enough to fit. I hauled half a bucket of cold water and poured it into the sink, then followed with hot water, one pitcher at a time, out of the pot on the stove. I had to move quickly because the water cooled fast. The sink was deep but narrow, and barely had enough space for a kid to sit in it while still being able to fill a cup with water to pour over them. An hour later all three kids were washed, dried, and dressed.

So much for dinner on time. It was too late to cook - the water in the buckets was barely above freezing, and heating it up on the camping stove burner took so long. The stove eye was tiny and inefficient at best, but with the water so cold it would take forever. Tonight we needed to simplify - we would have rice cakes, peanut butter, and bananas.

It was only 5:30, but it was pitch black outside. I hated when the sun went down so early in the winter - it made the long nights feel like a suffocating, shadowy prison. I lit the lantern and hung it on the outside nail. The light was dim and frustrated my sight, but I had to preserve the batteries on the headlamp, so I would work by its faint flame instead.

I fed the kids, cleaned up the mess, and laid them down for bed, continually feeding the fire in the meantime. I was too tired to wash the dishes but it would be harder in the morning, so I forced myself to do it anyway. Then came bringing enough wood in for the night and arranging it around the stove so it could continue to dry out. Semi-wet wood would make for a cold night.

As the night got darker and the lamp ran out of oil, the light dimmed, and so did my spirit. I took off the enthusiasm I faked during the day - like a dirty skirt tossed on the floor - and stared out into the middle of the room, at nothing. I was physically exhausted from the day, but my weariness was more than aching muscles and a sore back. My soul was tired.

18

DANDELIONS

I sunk the spade into the earth. It stopped an inch in. I sighed. This would take a long time. Removing the shovel, I repositioned and tried again, this time forcing it to go deeper. Using my foot, I kicked at the metal lip to drive it through the hard clay. I swayed the handle back and forth, loosening the dirt, then repeated the process from the other side of the dandelion.

I pulled at the base of the plant again, careful to not sever the root. The roots could be used for tea. It came out in one piece, with the delightful ripping sound a weed makes when being removed. I loved that sound. I carefully beat the plant against the shovel to knock the dirt off, and deposited it in the crumpled plastic bag. I was up to four plants.

We had run out of food. Devlin was not home as usual and had left me with no money. It was time to forage. That morning I had gone out and collected all the leftover popcorn heads that had fallen in the field over the summer. They were gnarly and oddly shaped, but they had seeds on them. Now that the stalks had died down, they were easier to see. We had harvested the popcorn earlier that year, but today I gleaned the lost heads. Afterwards I headed to the small round garden by the shed. I was able to find twelve rough-looking radishes, some split with age, but still edible, along with their leaves.

In the field where we had planted vegetables that summer, I foraged around where the carrots had been - perhaps there would be a few scraggly leftovers. Nope, not one. I did, however, find a lone wild onion. I pulled it up and headed back to the shed.

Dumping the bag of popcorn husks out onto a tray, I asked the girls if they would help pop the seeds off. They loved this job. I got busy on the dandelions, pinching the leaves from the root and tossing them into a bowl. I did the same with the radishes. At least we had enough water. Getting to the spring was not an option without money for gas to get there. Washing the dirt from the roots was extra laborious as I tried to desperately conserve water. We would need it for tea.

I set the radishes on a plate and smiled. I was happy, and a little proud, that I was able to find this much. Mae climbed up on her stool and peeked over the countertop. Eyeing the wild onion, she took her tiny finger and poked the bulb which wasn't much bigger than a pea.

"Mom, wook!"

"That's an onion your size, Mae!" Emma chirped.

I took the popcorn and tossed it into the pot. It was not easy to dry-pop it, as the kernels tended to burn before getting hot enough to explode, but I need to save the oil for the radish and dandelion leaves. If I got the proportions right, enough oil and salt would help cancel out their bitter taste.

As the stove got hot, the popcorn exploded into white puffs, like miniature clouds. I was glad for it, but it made my stomach get knots just thinking about it. We had had popcorn for too many meals as the food supply got low, and my stomach had a hard time digesting it.

I wondered if I could get the generator started one more time. Or start the car one more time. I needed to make a call to Devlin about money. He hadn't come through with any like he promised, and it could be days before he made any effort in that direction. It was strange, he could always pull money from the sky when he needed to, but I had to beg for it to happen. I thought we just didn't have money; I never thought he would be hiding it.

Devlin refused to let me get a cell phone, so I had to make a phone call through the computer. Since the computer battery would not hold a charge, I had to have electricity from the generator, or it was useless. When I had enough strength to yank the pull cord on the generator, sometimes I could get it started and plug the laptop into an extension cord - but it didn't happen often. It took so many tries and I simply wasn't strong enough. The other option was hooking up a power converter to my vehicle. I would pop the hood of the car and connect the converter clamps onto the car battery, then plug in the laptop and sit in the passenger seat to get online.

Connecting to the internet was a whole new ball of fun. We had a hotspot USB "jump drive" from Devlin's cell phone company, but the reception was terrible. I might get one bar of reception, but that was it. It took on average 10 tries to have enough connection to dial out. If I wasn't fast enough, the converter would overheat and shut off, crashing the computer and starting the whole process over again. Sometimes it took 30 minutes of attempts to make one phone call.

I always called Devlin. It never occurred to me to call someone else - someone who would actually help. I couldn't let anyone know we were in a bad situation. Devlin would become absolutely unraveled. He taught me that if anyone found out we were not "fine," our family would be in danger. Now, I realize what kind of danger. It wouldn't have been danger from the world, from church friends, authorities, or government agencies. It would have come from *him*.

19

SOMETIMES THE SKIES ARE SILENT

I focused intently on the spire of grass I had plucked up. It was a wide blade, perfect for positioning between two thumbs and using as a whistle.

But I didn't need a whistle today. Instead I shredded it, stripping long strands of fiber from its base, one by one, and tossing them to the ground. When I was stressed, I fiddled with my hands; it gave me a small degree of relief. I shredded grass, leaves, mulch - anything I could - carefully and systematically picking them apart into a pile of tiny pieces. Then I would stack pebbles from the gravel driveway, as I sat on the bottom step of the shed. Anything fiddly seemed to help.

My body was giving out. Throughout the many months of living in the shed, I had tried to worker smarter, not harder, but it was not possible to work "less hard." The labor was too heavy for my body. As my body broke down, so did my mental fortitude. I have heard that it is during times of exhaustion that we are again faced with battles we won long ago. They come back to haunt us, to taunt us, to portray themselves as real again. And sometimes we must actually fight them again. This time, I fought the hopelessness.

I was tired, *so* tired. I was too tired to move, too tired to breathe. I did not have energy to waste crying, but the tears came anyway. This time I did not hold them back. Hot streams of saltiness ran down my face. I needed help, wanted help. But the world only felt harder, and more brutal than ever.

A daddy-long-legs spider creeped over the edge of the step where I sat. He paused, as if deciding on his course, then marched smartly across the wood, as if on a mission. I watched him in silence. His spindly legs made him appear to bounce with each step. Even with his small size, he had more stamina than me, apparently.

It is the tiny details of the property I remember the clearest. The cracked, neon-green husks of the black walnuts, which fell prematurely from the trees due to drought. The spires of grass at the corner of the shed, the clumps of chickweed with their miniature white flower petals. The smooth feeling of worn-out rubber tires Devlin had removed from a vehicle and stacked nearby. The gritty copper-colored rust on disintegrating sheets of metal that lay all over the property.

I traced the shapes of nature with my fingers. I felt the roughness of tree bark, the slippery round pebbles of the creek bed. As an herbalist, I noticed the cone-shaped seed-heads waving above the plantain leaves, the soft fuchsia blossoms of red clover, and the heart-shaped papery seeds of yellow dock that grew prolifically in the summer. The tangled, knotted jungle of weeds that grew taller than my head were home to thousands of buzzing, flying insects which continually sprung in all directions. I watched the ants scurry around foraging, quickly for a moment, pausing for a few seconds, then scurrying again.

My mind soaked up these details, because they were simple - they required no thought or energy to absorb. It was by focusing on the nitty-gritty particulars of my surroundings that I survived the things which were not describable - the fear and dread I felt that did not yet have a name, the desperation and despondency that crept closer, like a deadly tide, every day.

I could never ignore my situation, or pretend I was somewhere else; my mind was confined to my surroundings. When I was younger, my thoughts were liberated enough to daydream, to soar above the harsh realities I faced, and for those few moments I could be free in spirit. Somehow, I had lost that ability. I felt incapable of breaking loose from the present - even for just a minute - to imagine a better future. It was as if I was too depleted to mentally rise above my circumstances anymore.

I wanted it to end. I did not want to die, but my fight to survive could not continue indefinitely. My hope was daily murdered by exhaustion. I was depleted of strength. My body craved rest so desperately, that to lie down and pray that God didn't allow me to wake up felt like the only respite I had left.

But my children.

They needed a mother. They were so little, so innocent. But how could I go on another day? I was *so tired.*

I have to fight.

But I had no fight left.

Please, God. I can't do this anymore. I just can't. Please help me, or put me out of my misery. I just...cannot... do this... another day.

Did He even hear? Did my prayers rise higher than my own prostrated heart?

God, please! I've never doubted Your existence, but I need You to hear me! I can't live like this anymore... PLEASE.

The skies were silent.

20

RUNNING OUT OF TIME

I was sick. Very sick. It was time to petition.

I rarely asked Devlin for anything. I had been treated like a captive slave for so long. What kind of beaten-down, despised slave asks for favors from his master? But if I didn't ask now, I wouldn't make it. I felt sick all the time. Something was wrong, but I didn't know what.

There were a lot of things going on in my body due to stress, but something else felt very "off." I was barely functioning. I felt like I was going to break any moment. It was hard to breathe. It was hard to move. I was down to 88 pounds with no muscle mass at all. I needed to rest.

By this time Devlin had started to transition his business to Tennessee. He had been coming home to the shed every night for a few months. When he got home that night, I timidly started my campaign to request help. There was an urgency I felt in my body that I needed changes, and I needed them fast.

I wanted to go to my sister's house to visit for a few weeks. She lived about an hour away. I thought maybe I just needed to have some time to rest and recuperate without doing all the hard, daily labor just to survive. Having electricity would make chopping and hauling firewood, and waking up all night to feed the wood stove just to stay warm, unnecessary. Hot running water for showers would eliminate hauling buckets of heavy water. A five-minute hot shower would feel SO good! Cooking would be a 10-minute ordeal instead of an hour and a half. I just…needed… rest.

Of course, that wasn't the pitch I threw to Devlin. He would shut down any plea for help if he thought I would be resting. Resting, in his book, was just laziness. I tried to make him understand how bad I felt. I was the strongest person I knew - able to tolerate well beyond what most people could handle, and then some. But even the strongest person can eventually break. For me to actually ask for help, meant that I was down for the count.

"Can I please go - just for like 2 weeks?" I really needed at least a month, but I knew he would never agree to that.

"Look, if you need help, then I can go to Atlanta and bring back some boxes of carrots and apples and stuff."

"For what?"

"For juicing."

"This isn't about juicing. I need things to let up just a little bit. I don't even have energy to do juicing right now. I can't do…one…more…thing right now."

I was getting desperate. His alternative was not an option. I couldn't stay in the shed anymore, I just couldn't. Something inside me knew that. Of course, he always thought that juicing was the answer to any health problem; from a pimple to cancer. My sickness was not a carrot deficiency. I needed a doctor and a diagnosis. And rest. Nutrition would have helped of course. I was protein and vitamin deficient and my caloric intake was negative compared to my output. But it would not be enough on its own.

"I just need a few weeks. She's only an hour away. I just

need some time to do some natural remedies, hard core, to get back to myself."

"Look, the thing that works best for feeling better is getting your circulation going. There have been so many times I've felt bad, but all I have to do is get up and force myself to get moving and I feel better. You probably just need to work harder. Like, go out and push the lawn mower for two hours. You'll sweat and you'll feel better. You probably aren't outside enough in the fresh air."

I probably just need to work harder?!?

I was stunned. I had heard stupid things from Devlin over the years, but this... this, I absolutely could not believe.

I could feel my body wilting. He was not interested in any option other than his.

Big surprise.

But I have to go. I *have* to. The feeling in my core was so strong it was almost vocal.

But there was nothing else to say. If he really thought I just needed to "work harder," nothing I said would be of any use. I dropped the subject. He was happy.

Two weeks passed. It seemed like forever. My mind was in a fog, my body giving out. I lifelessly did the daily things, but crept along. It was a strange time; I remember specifics, as clear as day, but I also felt I was in a dream - maybe the effects of adrenaline or cortisol.

At church, an event was mentioned; they were having a three-day seminar. I wanted to go. I wanted to be around other people. I wanted a break from daily survival, to be around something that gave me more life than what I possessed right then.

Devlin said I could go for one day, but that I didn't need to go for three. Something stirred within me. I am not sure what it was. I didn't care for the seminar *that* much, but I had such an urge to get away from the property and have a break, that I just needed to *go*. I decided I would plan to go for three days anyway. For some reason Devlin didn't prevent me from going to church activities - it was as if he felt God would punish him if he got in the way of "spirituality." Or maybe he just didn't want me to ever vocalize to any of the church members that he "wouldn't let me go." He never wanted to be looked down upon by outsiders - he had to keep up a good front.

I packed some clothes for the kids and a few other random things we might need. That night Devlin saw my preparations and was irritated at my subtle rebellion. I figured he was carefully weighing out the situation - potential exposure, versus me not being available to tend to his needs. There was another dynamic in the mix: He wanted to make sure I was going to *return*. He saw this as flight, and he would have none of it.

"Fine, go to the seminar. I will keep the children here, since they are such a burden to you."

"What?"

"Go to the church thing. I'll keep the kids here and take them to work with me on Sunday."

I stared at him. Taking the kids to his job site was not an option. He left live nail guns on the floor with buckets of bleach and industrial chemicals. He didn't watch them. If he actually did have to take them, I would be punished in the end for inconveniencing him. This was a trap I couldn't get out of. It was his way of making sure I didn't go to the seminar based on "my own choice."

"That doesn't even make sense."

"Well, you are the one who says your health is so bad because you never get a break. Now you'll have a break. You won't have to take care of your kids, since they are wearing you out *so* bad!"

"I never said they were -"

"Go! Do whatever you want!"

"I never said -"

"Yes, you did!"

I wanted to scream. I hated when my words were twisted. I was also way too tired to argue and fight anymore.

I'm not staying. Neither are they. He can fuss about this later.

The sick feeling in my mind and in my core made me bold. I was no longer rationalizing with myself about the danger of the fallout I would suffer. I had this "knowing" feeling it was more dangerous to stay. I just had to go.

In the early morning I got up, trying not to stir Devlin. I didn't want another argument. I didn't know whether to go to the seminar for three days or just to church for the day; sleep had changed my mind. I didn't feel strong enough to deal with the fallout. I decided I could make a final decision later in the day.

Emma was awake and getting dressed. I lifted the baby out of his bed and put him in his car seat. It was easier to have sleeping children on the way to church; I would dress him later. I got some fruit and crackers for breakfast to eat on the way.

Devlin got up.

"Where are you going?"

"Church."

"You're not taking the kids."

"What?"

My all-time, recycled answer.

"I told you last night you're not taking the kids."

"I didn't even say I was going to the seminar. I haven't even decided if I am staying yet. Right now I am going to church."

"Good, go to church. They are staying here. Go and do your seminar thing. I will take them to work on Sunday."

"Oh come on, that isn't going to work and you know it."

"Look, if you are so burdened by all your *hard work* you do around here, then go take your vacation!" he yelled, sarcastically spitting out the words "hard work."

Ridiculous.

I told Emma to get in the car, and picked Mae up.

Devlin moved towards me.

"I said NO."

Adrenaline shot through my body. He blocked the door.

"You aren't going anywhere."

What the heck!?

"*You* can go to church. You are not leaving this house with the kids. I am very serious. It's NOT happening."

I tried to move past him, and he used his body to block me, making a barricade between me and door. I would not win this one. The look on his face told me he was about to get violent. We would all get hurt.

Something shifted within me. I knew this feeling. It was that feeling of utter entrapment. He was blocking me in, there was no way out. To fight would mean instant defeat.

This cannot be happening! I haven't even done anything! What, I can't go to church now? Why is he acting like this?

Even more importantly, what was going to happen next? His face had melted into that furious calm which meant imminent danger. I had to recalculate. I had to protect my kids.

My mind was racing, while thoughts triggered deep within, worked their way to the surface.

I am not four years old anymore. I am bigger and smarter than I was then. You may have me trapped now, but you will not forever.

I sat down on the bed.

"Fine, I'm not going. I'll stay here."

I kicked my shoes off, indicating my intent. There was no way I was leaving the kids with an angry man on the edge of violence. I would stay put.

"No, you are going to go!" Devlin demanded.

"No, forget it. It's not worth all this. I'll just stay here."

I sat on the bed, staring out the window for a while. Devlin's shoulders relaxed, but he did not move away from the door.

What am I going to do? What CAN I do? What...next?

Thoughts swirled in my head in circles. I tried to fixate on one at a time, but none of them stood still long enough. My brain was furiously scanning, scanning for answers. Devlin moved two feet over towards the counter, guarding the door, ever ready to pounce. He was playing the "fake it" game, trying to pretend nothing was out of the ordinary.

I need to get help. I need to go.

If I left, I could get help. I stood up.

"Fine. Keep them here. I'm going to church."

Devlin moved back towards the door, blocking me again. He cocked his head and looked at me suspiciously. He studied me, staring me down as if reading my brain. Then he spoke.

"Okay. But you are not going alone. I am going too."

Again, stunned.

This makes no sense.

My gut knew it made sense, however. He thought I was going to run, or that I was going to go get help. That wasn't going to work for him. He needed to control all the variables. He had to make sure I wasn't going to "tattle" on him.

"Okay, whatever."

I played the everything-is-normal game too. I got Mae dressed and ready for church just like it was any other week, except this time Devlin would be going with us, which he normally didn't do. We drove to church, mostly in silence. We would continue the everything-is-fine game for a good portion of the morning. We showed up at church and sat through Bible study class, pretending everything was fine. Church service was like every other typical week. Afterwards there was church potluck. Devlin was watching me like a hawk. He wanted to see who I would talk to. I felt like a criminal in a jumpsuit, being watched by a prison guard. I smiled, said hello to people, collected the children from their class. Went to the bathroom. As people were going through the lunch line and sitting down at tables, I casually started chatting with my friend, Nikki. I laughed and acted like we were chatting about something benign. I slowly turned toward her with my back facing towards Devlin.

"Don't look anywhere but my face right now. Smile like everything is fine. Really, *nothing* is fine."

She smiled.

"No matter what you do, do not look at Devlin right now. He is watching my every move and watching every single person I am talking to. Things are really, really bad right now."

I was still smiling. She smiled too. She was smart like that.

"He blocked me in the house today and wouldn't let me leave. He thinks I am trying to run or something, I don't know. He wouldn't let me out with the kids. Then when I decided to come to church myself, he insisted he was coming too. Something is way off."

She got the gist. She had been a social worker before. She knew the signs that things were NOT well.

"Did he hurt you?"

"No...not exactly. He just barricaded himself against the

door and wouldn't let me out. Trapped. Emma was crying and yelling that she wasn't going to stay with him, that she was 'Going to go with Mama!' She knew something was way off because he has never prevented us from leaving before."

"No child should have to be scared like that."

"I know."

I have no idea how the rest of the conversation went after that, but she told me that if I needed to call her, day or night, she would be there. She assured me of this.

I have someone on my team. I have promise of help.

That was enough. I calmed down. I had someone who believed me and would help me. I wasn't crazy. Things would get better.

I went home that night. I didn't know *why* it would be okay, but I knew it would be okay. I didn't know the drastic changes that would be coming, but I knew I didn't have to do it alone. That made all the difference.

21

WHEN THE DECISION IS MADE FOR YOU

He came home like a storm cloud. He must have had a bad day at work. Tonight, he would take it out on me. I don't remember the details of what led up to his explosion, but he blamed it on a spoon. Or rather the lack of a spoon.

I was getting the children settled into bed when he arrived. Maybe he was mad because all the attention wasn't on him, or maybe because I didn't have a three-course meal laid out for him. It probably had nothing to do with me, but I mentally ticked through the options of the things that he usually got mad about and blamed me for. I laid down on the bed to nurse the baby to sleep - maybe that was it - I didn't "appear" to be busy. Devlin hated it when he thought I was being lazy, and therefore inconvenienced to do stuff he believed was "women's work." Like fetching him a spoon.

He was hungry and asked what was for dinner. I pointed to half a loaf of bread and some tomatoes that were sitting stoically in a bowl on the counter. This was his favorite combination. He usually cut the tomatoes up and made a "tomato salad" - drenching them in olive oil and salt and ate them with a spoon just like that. He was usually happy with the bread "as-is" - pinching off pieces from the loaf as he ate. That's how they did it in Romania.

But today he wanted the tomatoes already cut for him - it wasn't *ready*. He had given me no clue when he was planning to arrive home. If the tomatoes were cut too soon, they would get mushy and attract the flies. I could never win.

He tossed his binder and plastic bag full of lunch dishes on the floor in a huff and disappeared outside - where the sink was - to get a knife and a spoon. He had moved the sink out of the shed and into the yard some months ago, for a reason I never figured out. It was harder for me to wash them out there, because the sun rays reflected off the metal, causing a painful glare, and radiating heat - as if I needed more of that! Maybe he moved it out *because* it was harder for me; he no longer pretended to care about my well-being - his animosity had grown. He was increasingly hostile by the day.

I stroked the baby's head, straightening his soft wisps of hair, and arranging them around his face. He was dozing off.

I heard a crash of dishes. A frightening, intentional smashing of glass. Devlin was shattering them in the sink. Dread arose in my gut instantly, making my stomach churn and causing my heart to race. I curled my body around the baby, bracing for a potential assault. I wasn't aware what he was mad about, but it didn't matter - once he was angry all bets for safety were off.

He stomped up the steps and flung the door open, raging about how there was "not one single spoon in the entire house" that was clean.

It was possible. We were down to only 1-1/2 gallons of water which I had saved for drinking. Devlin had his own water supply at work, but the children and I had to share that last bit between all of us. We had to have water to drink. The dishes had to wait, or be washed in creek water.

I had never seen him this angry. He was yelling like a madman, and I started shaking. My body, tense with terror, felt like it was going in reverse. I felt nauseous. I didn't dare move. His volatility was at a peak.

He stomped back outside, slamming the door with such force the whole building shook. I heard more dishes being slammed around in the sink, and smashed. And this silent little voice whispered in my ear, so clear it was almost audible.

"He can't *hear* you."

An indescribable, but extremely powerful voice. It thundered through my head with the intensity of dynamite and clarity as sharp as glass. In that moment, deep in my gut I understood that those words meant so much more than a mere referral to Devlin's auditory senses.

He couldn't hear me - he was completely insensible to my sickness or frailty. He was deaf to our pain, and blind to our suffering. He would not only *not* hear my pleading for help to save my life - but he absolutely did not care about our welfare. If I didn't get out, I would die here. Devlin would not spare me.

I wasn't ready to die. It was time to leave.

There was absolutely no question in my mind that I needed to get out, *immediately*. Something about Devlin's demeanor and those words spoken to my innermost core, awakened an urgent need for flight. Something was very wrong, and I didn't know what, but somehow my soul did.

My nervous system was thrown into emergency mode. I

dry heaved and shook uncontrollably. Devlin eventually went to bed, probably satisfied that he had affected me so much, and hoping I had learned my lesson. I sat on the edge of the bed near the wood stove, trying to get warm and sipping water with herbs, hoping it would calm my stomach and tension enough that I could lay down.

I stayed awake for many hours, halfway in shock. I had no plan. I only knew that flight needed to be imminent. I eventually fell into a fitful sleep, never really reaching full unconsciousness.

In the morning, Devlin piddled around getting ready for work. The tension in the air was so thick it could be cut with a knife. He stalled in going to work. He must have felt that something big was about to happen. Maybe he thought I would tell others what had happened. He delayed, slowing his preparation down to a snail's pace. I slowly did my morning routine, avoiding his gaze. He finally said goodbye and looked at me expectantly. I couldn't look at him. He shrugged his shoulders, but his face was anything but nonchalant - more like a combination of fear and anger - irritation perhaps from being susceptible to exposure?

I waited about 30 minutes after he drove away before springing into action. I expected him to turn around and come back to the house to check out our activities. He was sly that way, when he wanted to catch people. I counted on him showing up at any moment.

I called my friend Nikki and prayed she would answer. With every ring, I willed harder.

Come on!

No response.

I looked around the room and started mindlessly dividing belongings. I had to get the most crucial things, but I was not sure what those were - I was in a fog of panic and adrenaline.

I could not pile things on the bed or counter; if Devlin

came back I would be caught. Everything had to look normal. I opened a cabinet and divided the items into two sides: needs on the right, leave-behind things on the left, then closed the door again. I opened the next cabinet and did the same, separating items to the left or right. I needed to be sure to get the essentials. I had to pack as if I was never coming back.

My intention was not to leave my marriage, or Devlin. At that time, it was only to survive. I needed a place for the winter with heating, electricity, and water. I was not strong enough to haul buckets anymore, I could not chop any more wood. I could not physically do the things to keep us alive for several more months. My body was broken.

I knew, however, that Devlin would take this as the world's worst betrayal, and that he would very possibly file for divorce and leave me permanently. I had to be prepared for that very real probability. Devlin never forgave an offense. One of this magnitude he would carry forever, and I would become a target of the worst revenge. I always knew this deep down, though my conscious mind had me convinced that he loved me. Such a strange web of lies victims believe! It is curious and infuriating how we believe the stories our abusers tell us!

I called Nikki again, this time she answered. Relief flooded my body.

"I need to get out! Today! Now!"

She was silent. Then, "What?"

I hadn't given her much of a heads up.

"I need to get out now. I can't wait. I have to get out now before he comes home!"

She could hear the panic and urgency in my voice. I was not exaggerating, something was very wrong. She promised to come right away. I thanked her and hung up.

I grabbed the box of twigs and branches used to start the fires in the wood stove. They rattled to the floor as I dumped them out in a pile, and I used the empty box to put the kids' clothes in. I scooted the box towards the foot of the mattress and covered it with a blanket. I continued grabbing items and arranging them in a particular way that would make loading them into Nikki's van easy and fast, yet looking as natural as possible. I prayed with every cell in my body that Devlin would not show up. I had no backup plan if he did.

Nikki eventually arrived and we had her van loaded in minutes. I was desperate to get out, knowing even a few seconds made a difference. There was only one way in and one way out of the property. Five seconds could make the difference between escape, or being blocked in by Devlin's approaching van.

Nikki wanted to make sure nothing was left behind that I would need.

"Let's *go*!" I begged.

"What about toys for the kids?"

She was thinking about things that would make things easier for me in the long run (keeping them occupied when I couldn't), and helping to lessen the stress on them (being surrounded by familiar toys might help) but I just wanted to *leave*. Terror was overwhelming me.

"Forget it! We *need to go*."

She collected some toys anyway.

"Okay, I think we're set."

Thank God!

I secured the kids in their car seats in my car and slammed the door.

I took a deep breath. There was one more thing I forgot.

I ran back in the shed, grabbed a scrap of paper and scribbled four words on it. I paused for a few seconds, reading it over, then placed it right in the middle of the empty counter. I ran outside and jumped in the driver's seat. We were leaving, and I couldn't get out of there soon enough.

He would find the note when he returned home. Maybe it would soften the blow and protect us from the flood of fury I knew he would soon unleash. If there was any hope, it might be in that small scribble:

"I still love you."

22

WHEN NOWHERE IS SAFE

I had no plan. I had nowhere to go. I hadn't *planned* on where to go or what to do. Life had not come with instructions, and nobody had sat me down at some point in my youth and told me "If you are ever in a domestic abuse situation and you need to get out, you need to sit down and make a safety plan."

My boat may have been on fire, but now I had jumped into a vast ocean, without a life jacket, not realizing I couldn't swim. Thankfully I had a friend with me who was able to help brainstorm options. I called the women's shelter first and the lady who answered asked me some questions. One of them was "Did he hit you?"

"No."

"Well, our shelter is primarily for women fleeing abusive situations where their partners have hit them."

She might have been a new employee and didn't ask all the questions. I am sure if I explained my situation fully to her, she would have given me other options, but I didn't see myself as a "battered woman" or even a woman fleeing her husband. I didn't see myself as an abused wife and I definitely didn't have the words to describe my situation. Maybe I should have put Nikki up to the task of calling.

I spent the first night at a hotel. I should have known better. But I could not go to Nikki's house - it would be the first place Devlin would look. So she stayed at the hotel with us, as a support, through that first hard night.

I made the mistake of parking my car in front of the door of my hotel room. It hadn't occurred to me to hide it. At 11 p.m. there was a knock on the door. Nikki and I froze, looking at each other with big eyes. We were silent.

The knock came again.

There was no spy-hole on the door to be able to see who it was. Nikki silently picked up the phone receiver and dialed the front desk. She pulled the phone base as far towards the bathroom as possible, resting it on the bed, then stretched the springy phone cord and pulled the receiver into the bathroom.

Four rings later they answered.

"Somebody is knocking on our door and we cannot see out. Would that be anyone from the front desk?"

"No ma'am, nobody from up here would be at your room. Would you like us to check on it for you?"

"Yes, please."

"Okay, we will be over there in a moment." Nikki hung up.

"The front desk is going to come see!" she mouthed, in a barely-audible whisper. We sat, frozen and on edge, waiting as the seconds slowly ticked by.

Silence.

Silence can strangely feel like torture.

Several minutes later, Nikki called the front desk again, hoping for an update.

"Yes, ma'am, there was a guy outside your door. He was walking away from the building when I approached him. A really skinny guy with an accent. He didn't have a vehicle, he just walked away towards another parking lot." A perfect description of Devlin.

The next morning I left the hotel, and went into hiding for the next three weeks. It would take that long to get an apartment. Prior to leaving the shed, a friend had promised to help fund an apartment for the winter, as she had a feeling I wasn't going to live otherwise. Though I didn't know it then, several people had seen my health deteriorate so much that none of them thought I would live through the winter without some sort of intervention. Collaborating together, they helped with expenses of shelter, food, and gas to get around.

It was a terrible time. Those four little words on the note had apparently done nothing to ease the insult of my flight. Devlin was on the war path and I was the target and so was everyone associated with me.

He went to the sheriff and made a complaint that I had "kidnapped" his children. He started calling up the last people I had called (he got from a call list from the cell phone company) and started threatening them. He declared they had committed a crime and were going to be "very, very sorry." He made threats of sending police to their homes. He called up people in the church and told his victim story. He left voicemails for me telling me to contact him immediately asking if we could "calmly discuss some issues," and then minutes later sent more threatening messages to my friends. He was so angry he couldn't even hide his obvious duplicity.

I took some general precautions for safety. I avoided common places like Walmart where I might run into him. Everywhere I went, I watched the roads, looking for his van everywhere. I took random backroads to get to destinations.

It was about 6 weeks before I met up with him again, face to face. He smoothed things over, and told me the things I wanted to hear - that he loved me and couldn't live without me. That he wanted what was best for us. That we needed to work things out and build our house and raise our children together. I fell for it, not noticing that he had not even apologized for his behavior. I wanted to believe things would be okay.

After all, he wasn't a bad guy. He just did stupid stuff.

I never moved back to the shed, but I "went back" to the relationship. I was naive - extremely naive. When I had left the property, I knew to expect potentially crazy behavior, but I didn't take into consideration *what it said about him as a person*. He was intentionally deceitful, devious, malicious. But I had been brainwashed for so many years. I overlooked it as "what he does when he is stressed out." I justified his threats and lies because he had told me so many times that he loved me. I didn't even know what love was. It is ironically true that usually the last person to recognize abuse for what it is, is the victim, and this was true in my situation. It wasn't intentional blindness, but rather a combination of the results of victimization, trauma-bonding, and a heck of lot of conditioning.

Freedom is a funny thing. Ultimately, we are only as free as our minds allow. Regardless whether we are chained up or physically restrained, our minds can soar above our bonds. The tricky thing about domestic violence, is that even though you may be physically free, you can still be bound by beliefs that are far more imprisoning than outward circumstances are.

I would spend the next 4-1/2 years trying to reconcile

with Devlin for this very reason. I believed in marriage. I believed I should keep our family intact. I believed I should keep us together "for the kids' sake." I believed divorce was wrong and remarriage was forbidden. I didn't believe I could ever make it on my own. I was devastated I might have to hand my kids over to a public school or babysitter "to raise" instead of being a homeschooling stay-at-home mom. I thought all the important things in life would be lost. All these thoughts ate away at me and convinced me that staying was the best option.

Devlin continued to live in the shed during this time, with alterations for his comfort of course (electricity, phone, and internet for starters). He started to build onto the shed and made himself a tiny kitchen and washing area. I lived at the apartment with the children. He had decided to tread more carefully now that "other people" were involved in my welfare. He had to preserve his reputation as much as possible after all, if he wanted to eventually suck me back in. He could not look bad to everyone else, or they might influence me to "put my foot down." He couldn't afford that. He would allow me to live at the apartment for several months before he started pressuring me to move back to the shed.

Things initially seemed to improve, but nothing ever really changed for the better. What he did get better at was hiding his intentions and anger. He got better at hiding the abuse. He got better at manipulating me and explaining things away. I was put on some kind of emotional probation with him. After all, *I* was the one who had broken his trust, he said. He would dole out minimal affection depending on how nice and compliant I was to his wishes. If I would fail in some aspect of marriage in his eyes, he would withdraw from me and subtly hint at abandonment - his way of triggering me into obedience. While he had always done this, he now used my "betrayal" as his reasoning and way of gaining leverage to dominate more.

I justified many of his attacks. I told myself he was just wounded - that he felt rejected, and that wounded people hurt other people. I knew that I hadn't done anything wrong, but he had somehow internalized that I did, so to him, it was "real." I couldn't argue with something that was "real" to him, no matter how fabricated.

I tried my best to win his trust back. I shouldered the burden of fixing our relationship. I bought a save-your-marriage program and went through it faithfully, and engulfed myself in its principles for two solid years. I read every article on marriage the internet could provide. I read oodles of marriage books on respect, trust, and love, and all the "languages of love" that I needed to pay attention to so that I could communicate with Devlin in a way he understood. I self-diagnosed him as a workaholic who needed help, but who I knew wasn't really interested in changing. I resigned myself to a life as a wife of a work addict and tried to find ways to cope.

It was hardly a life. I couldn't act like a single parent, making decisions for our family that I thought would help us keep our heads above water, but I couldn't act married either, as Devlin simply wouldn't engage. He came up to visit us at the apartment one day a week, sometimes every week but often only every other week, and he came on the day he was religiously forbidden to work; otherwise, we probably never would have seen him. He ruled us from afar, calling to instruct us how to live and what to do.

While I had more freedom in the apartment when he was gone than I had on the property, he would sometimes show up with little or no warning if he wanted to get a shower, a hot meal, his clothes washed, or to get his sexual needs met. So I had to live as if he was still in charge. Within a year of escaping, he had me completely dependent on him again. He took over paying the rent after six months because he didn't want me "being dependent on friends" and said it was "his responsibility to do that."

I tried my hardest to make the best life for us I could, but I was losing ground. Devlin started creating issues that forced me to make decisions. He wanted me to move back to the property. I tried to discuss it with him, but I ultimately refused until he could arrange a decent living situation. He told me I was requiring too much - that wanting a toilet and a bath to wash the kids was unreasonable. He wanted to get a loan (in my name since he was illegal) for $80,000 to build our house and said that I needed to get on board and sign the papers or he would stop paying the rent on my apartment. I refused that too, knowing that he would squander the money, but also afraid of what he would do if I didn't. What would I do if he stopped paying the rent? We would obviously be kicked out.

Life got increasingly complicated. As I felt things falling apart, I occasionally wondered what would happen if we ended up divorced. I didn't believe in divorce, so I could not even visualize a life that included it. But I also knew things could not continue indefinitely - I felt it, and my gut feeling had never been wrong. I had been taught to never trust feelings - the church said that they would lead you astray and into sin. Feelings were "deceitful and wicked" and I had been taught to bury my gut feeling. Yet somehow that intuitiveness had not died out completely. It was buried, but not dead. It helped prepare me for the things that were coming.

23

AND THEN, SOME OF US HOLD OUR ORGANS

Most people who knew, called me brave. Inwardly I laugh, because I know the truth. The reality was, I was just terrified of the alternatives.

My children were born at home, unassisted. No midwife, no doctor, no assistant. I didn't think much of it. It was just another fact of life, another decision I had made contrary to "normal."

There were people who used the word "brave" as a compliment, and those who used it as a substitute for "stupid," so as not to be offensive. I could tell by the look on their face what they really meant.

I originally made the choice because of well-concealed fear. I had heard too many stories. I knew about the 30% Cesarean-section rate, the epidurals and episiotomies gone wrong. I had heard the birth stories of friends, detailing unnecessary interventions they had experienced at hospitals, and I didn't want the same. Then, there was the elderly woman I knew, who sat me down and explained how for 40 years she defecated through her vagina regularly because her doctor had cut her during birth and did not sew her up properly afterwards. To say I was apprehensive about a hospital birth, would have be an understatement. "Terrified" would have described it better.

Because of the Georgia state law forbidding midwives to attend home births, I either had to find an underground midwife, willing to risk jail time if something went wrong, or prepare my own do-it-yourself birth. I chose the latter; it was more feasible. In my defense, I was young, hopeful and, well, "brave."

The births of our first three children were fairly uneventful. Devlin pretty much left me to my own devices during labor, and would come around when the baby was actually being born. I mostly labored alone while he surfed the internet. I didn't expect anything else from him by the time baby #4 was on the way. I had already been trained to accept his distance and apathy.

Levi's birth however, was different. I knew I needed help, even during pregnancy. My body had been weakened from living in the shed, and although we were living in the apartment by that time, I did not have the stamina for another birth, physically or mentally. I wanted a midwife. I wanted help.

It was not to be. Now in Tennessee, it was legal to have a midwife at a home birth, but Devlin refused to fund one. After all, I had done this three times already; I couldn't waste our money on something "unnecessary." And then there was the control issue. Devlin was a fighter. If a midwife was present, it took the control away from him. If she would make a suggestion Devlin didn't like, a fight would ensue. I knew I could not handle conflict while in labor.

I finally convinced him to allow an older woman from church to come and help. I deliberately chose someone he viewed as "submissive" and formulated my argument carefully.

"Cheryl could be another set of hands," I suggested.

He eventually relented. It was a small victory for me.

Levi was born in August, after a hot and humid summer. His labor was short - a little over two hours is what I tell people. Other than that, everybody gets a different version of the story.

I tell friends that he was born fast, without much break between contractions. Acquaintances hear about my obsession with cucumbers and watermelon during the last few weeks leading up to his birth. I hide the real story that I held my own organs in my hands. Nobody gets that version, it sounds insane. Maybe it is. Not many people get to do that and live to tell about it, I guess.

The reality was, Levi was born quickly and without much time for preparation. When labor started, Devlin stalled around, not calling Cheryl when I asked him to, because he didn't want "interference" any sooner than necessary. He then disappeared to go watch a DVD with the other kids, and I was alone as usual. When Levi's birth was imminent, the typical supplies had not been laid out. The blankets and medical supplies and container for the afterbirth were somewhere on the other side of the house. Watching Planet Earth was more important to Devlin than preparing for another baby.

I squatted on the bathroom floor, leaning heavily against the sink for support, unable to do anything for myself besides survive the relentless contractions. I pressed my head against the cold sink counter, breathing desperate pleas to God to make the agony stop. Time stood still. The shooting pain engulfed me. Devlin eventually came in and sized up the situation. He left, then returned with a plastic medical pad to lay out on the floor in just enough time for Levi to crown.

This time, however, there were complications. The placenta would not detach. It came out part of the way, then stopped, refusing to budge another centimeter. So I held it in my bare hand, cradling it against my body – one and a half pounds of what the medical community would describe as "beefy red tissue," or what the British might call "a bloody mess." I, on the other hand, called it a potential medical emergency, knowing that if it did not detach on its own, or if it tore in half in the process, it could lead to hemorrhage, infection, or in the worst-case scenario, death. Time was of the essence.

No matter, though - there was a knock at the door. Leaving me to figure out a solution on my own, Devlin left to go answer it.

Cheryl had arrived, along with her husband Frank, who had apparently come along as her driver. They walked into the living room, exchanging hellos with Devlin as he announced the baby had just been born.

I don't think there are words to describe that moment. I have tried hard to find the correct labels, but they fail me. There are not words to express certain levels of insanity and humiliation.

Devlin had left the bathroom door wide open and I was on display - half kneeling, half squatting on the bathroom floor, naked, bloody, and holding a dripping organ, in front of my friend and her husband. Exposed, humiliated, vulnerable.

Awkward. It was awkward.

The baby lay squirming on the bathroom floor. That was where Devlin had left him. I couldn't hold him – couldn't even reach him. I was shackled by a placenta which I was desperately trying to support, to avoid causing my innards to prolapse. The pool of blood got larger.

It took about 15 minutes and some careful maneuvering on my part, to coax the placenta to detach. After that, I don't remember much. I have flashback memories only of specific things. I wondered how I was going to get to my bedroom in a bath towel without Frank seeing me, since the only way to get there was through the living room. I wondered how I was going to avoid leaving a trail of blood through the house, on the carpet. Eventually I had to convince myself I didn't care about either. I had to get to bed, as the intensity of labor and the emotional drain left me debilitated, and I could no longer support my own body weight. I made a beeline to my room and collapsed on the bed, exhausted. I couldn't move. I stared at the little white string of Christmas lights I had wound around the nightstand. I fixated on their glow, to numb the pain, the emotions, the exhaustion, and the feelings of overwhelm. I could do nothing else. Someone cut the umbilical cord and brought Levi to me and I snuggled up with him and tried to block everything else out. Being "brave" had taken its toll.

"You threw it in the dumpster?!"

"What was I supposed to do?"

I didn't have an answer. I just knew that tying an organ up in a plastic bag and tossing it in the apartment dumpster was probably breaking every sanity code in the county.

Nice. Real nice.

Just another day in the life of the insane.

24

SNAPPING POINT

Everyone has a snapping point. Normal people. Psychopaths. Even the most holy and patient of saints. Even Jesus had his snapping point when he flipped tables upside down in the church (Matthew 21:12). What that snapping point looks like is different for each person. Some people have a mental breakdown. Others start yelling and throwing dishes. Some plot murder.

With an abuser you don't know which one you are dealing with. There are the kind of people who are like a simmering pot that gradually boils harder until it suddenly overflows. Then you have the pressure-cooker kind - the ones you always have to watch because you never know when an extreme explosion will come. They should wear a warning sign that says "Contents always under pressure. Stay away!"

I got unlucky with a two-in-one deal. Devlin was both a boiling pot and pressure cooker, and that changed daily, so it was anyone's guess what was in store for the day. Devlin feasted on power like a ravenous wolf, and he could never get enough of it. He would prove who was boss, as if his existence was dependent on it. "Discipline" was his way of establishing his dominance and satisfying his craving for control. He called the beatings "discipline." He called the suffocation "discipline."

Levi was 5 months old. He was tired because it was past his nap time. I was only gone for a minute to go to the bathroom. Devlin snatched this opportunity to feed his ego with the heart of a little baby. It would be a power struggle. He held him tight against his body, in a sitting position, but bent at the waist at about 45 degrees. No child sits comfortably like that on a good day. He started wailing. This was fodder for the fight. I returned from the bathroom.

"What are you doing? Give him to me!"

I was so frustrated! This was a simple fix. Levi needed a clean diaper, a soft blanket, and a dark room. He would be asleep in five minutes. He had proven it again and again.

"No, he isn't going anywhere until he gets this rebellious spirit out of him."

"Oh good grief! He's exhausted! It's his nap time. He needs to go to sleep."

Devlin would not budge. This would be an all-out war.

I grabbed Levi underneath his arms around his chest and tried to pull him out of Devlin's hands. Devlin tightened his grip and pulled away from me, like an angry child who was getting his teddy bear taken away.

"No! He's not going anywhere. I've had enough of this foolishness."

The baby screamed. Devlin squeezed tighter.

"What are you trying to prove? He's tired! What is he supposed to do?"

Rational thinking was never on Devlin's agenda.

"Tired or not, he is going to learn that he doesn't get his way by screaming."

He took his hand, which was almost bigger than Levi's entire face, and covered his mouth and nose to silence him.

I lunged.

"STOP! He can't breathe!"

I fought to rip his hand off. He pulled away from me again.

"HE CAN'T BREATHE WHEN YOU COVER HIS MOUTH AND NOSE!" I screamed.

What the heck was WRONG with him!?

"Then he will have to stop the screaming."

Devlin now moved to his calm phase of anger, when he became the most dangerous. He was decided. He would do whatever it took.

I can never forget the look of my baby in that moment. His eyes, big as saucers, locked eyes with mine, as he struggled with every ounce of energy in his body against the weight of the full-grown man who held him down.

Mama, help! HELP!

It was a look of sheer terror and desperation.

I attacked Devlin, grabbing his hand and prying his fingers off Levi's delicate face, while trying not to injure the baby in the process. He pulled away again, blocking me with one arm while holding tightly to Levi. I would not win this one. I simply was no match for him. He daily lifted construction materials that weighed more than me and could hold both my hands behind my back with just one of his.

There is no feeling as helpless as a mother who cannot protect her babies. Nevertheless, I fought. I have no idea how long the power struggle lasted, but minutes ticked by with me fighting for my son to breathe, and Devlin again attempting to cover his mouth and nose to prevent any future wails. It was a battle no mother, or child, should ever have to face.

Finally, he pushed me away and regained his composure. Feeling triumphant that he had "won," he sat up straight and let his hand drop from Levi's face. Levi sucked in air like a drowning creature just rescued from the water. He didn't have energy to scream because he could not get air fast enough. This time I grabbed for him, Devlin relented and let me take him. He was satisfied that we had all "learned our lesson."

The other children were crying in the corner, afraid of what just happened. It was just as much a lesson for them, as it was for me. "I am in control," was his lesson to us, "Don't ever question that."

My adrenaline surging, I carried Levi into the bedroom and calmed him down, keeping an ear tuned in to Devlin and the other children. I hoped I wouldn't have to prevent another outbreak, but I was on high alert, expecting it. Sure enough, five minutes later Levi was asleep.

Devlin had done this with every child, but never this young and never this long. For years I would never have called him "violent" because he swore up and down that everything he did was just a "child training" issue. It had nothing to do with abuse, but everything to do with "training children to obey" and if you "spare the rod, you spoil the child." He blamed my lack of consistent discipline on the reason he had to overcompensate to make them obey; I wasn't doing my job properly. I should have complete control over them at all times.

The church, although not as verbal about it as other topics, supported the mentality of complete control of children. The word "obedience" was synonymous with "holiness," and of course anything *not* holy would never be in heaven. Demanding strict obedience was a salvational issue if you wanted your family to be saved. Obedience to parents was equivalent to obedience to God, and the reverse was also true: Willing disobedience showed a rebellious, wicked heart.

I had no idea how you were supposed to gain strict obedience from children, so I tried different things:

spankings, time-outs, denying the coveted thing (such as a toy) until there was a better attitude, etc. It felt like a power struggle was going on, constantly. My children were small, and reasoning at that age was pretty much pointless. They didn't care for the moral reason it "wasn't okay" to smack their sibling in the head, or any one of the other hundreds of ridiculous things kids do. I felt I always lacked the know-how of what to do next. I knew, however, what was NOT okay, and regardless of church indoctrination or spousal abuse, when Devlin hit the kids, my maternal instinct kicked in. I was having none of it.

The strongest memory I have of Micah being abused was when he was around 7 years old. I wasn't even home when it happened. Devlin had refused for years to come to church, and at this period of our life we had worked out a deal. I would take the kids with me to church one week, and the next week they would stay at my apartment with Devlin who would come up to visit.

I could not miss the purple marks on Micah's face the moment I got home. They were in the perfect shape of a hand - Devlin's hand. He had hit him so hard, it had left a bruise in the shape of his hand as the blood vessels had burst. I didn't need to ask what had happened - it was too clear.

Devlin immediately started making excuses for why he hit him, telling me Micah had been out of control and needed discipline, and other typical ridiculous reasons that he normally gave. My eyes narrowed and I got quiet. I finally spoke.

"If you EVER hit him again, that will be the last mistake you make."

I wasn't kidding. I didn't need to say much more. I never talked to him that way and he was taken aback. He gave me a look that revealed he knew he had crossed my line.

The problem was, he didn't stop the abuse - he just got

better at hiding it from me. The only time I was away from the kids was when I went to church. When I would come home, everything seemed "fine." He would time his violent outbreaks for right after I had left the house, so by the time I returned, the kids would have had enough time to "calm down."

I would not find out about the extent of the abuse until years later when my kids finally told me. I was shocked and devastated. The hardest part was when my 12-year-old looked into my eyes and said "I thought you knew. And I thought you were okay with it."

All the marital advice I had ever read about never arguing in front of your kids had apparently backfired. Because I always argued with him behind closed doors, she thought we were united on what Devlin called "discipline," and she believed I was in agreement with the abuse inflicted on them.

I was speechless and heartbroken. All the fighting I had done to protect them, they had not seen or understood. They had felt unprotected and alone.

Never again. Come hell or high water, never again!

25

WHEN IT FINALLY HAS A NAME

I remember the day it finally had a name. I read the words in black and white - my story, almost verbatim. Except I hadn't written the article. I was confused. There was no denying the tactics. There was no denying the patterns. To the *detail,* this was my story. And they called it verbal abuse.

How could what he did be "abuse"? He loved me. Abusers don't love people - they *hurt* people. I couldn't call him an abuser. It didn't fit with my vision of him. For three days I sat in a state of shock. Call it a truth-bomb from God.

Maybe it seems incomprehensible, but in all the 12 years of being with Devlin, I never knew I was abused. I knew I was miserable. I knew I was sad. I knew that something felt very, very wrong. But I didn't know it was abuse. Perhaps this is why the first thing that abusers do is effectively take away your "voice." It is so you can't tell others what is going on.

I ruminated on this new information, rolling it over and over in my mind. In one sense, it was a relief - I wasn't crazy... other people went through this... and it had a name!

Fifteen names to be exact, as the article broke down into sections the fifteen different versions of verbal abuse: the discounting, undermining, accusing and blaming, withholding, and abuse disguised as a joke. Trivializing, name calling, diverting... Devlin did them all. I finally understood why our conversations were so exhausting and confusing to me! It wasn't me after all!

Conversations with him had never been logical or linear. He was a master at word salad - presenting unrelated ideas and arguments all tangled together. A rational person will try to find a logical thread between Point A, B and C, to ultimately gain a clear understanding of what the other person is saying. Devlin's goal, however, was to cause confusion, particularly when he was being challenged or held accountable for his actions. He would bring up completely unrelated points, acting as if they were connected to each other.

He would start off by making meaningless statements about people in general, their faults, the evils of the world, etc., then tie it into the matter at hand, deflect, blame, bring in completely unrelated topics, and ask irrelevant questions which left me (and others) wondering "What is he even talking about?"

He would then throw out a challenge to "prove him wrong" and get a triumphant look on his face as if he had already won. Conversation to him was a competition, to see how well he could confuse everyone. The article was a *huge* wake-up call.

Of course, the very next question that came to my mind was, *Does he know he does this?*

I *had* to know! So, in complete naivety, I asked him that very question the next time I saw him. How dumb can you get?

He answered my question with a question of his own. I

asked again. He deflected. I brought the conversation back around to my question. He discounted the issue. Then the denial and countering started. Within two minutes, he used 8 different types of verbal abuse. I stood there, in shock.

Finally I spoke, telling him up front what he had just done.

"First, you answered my question with a question. Then you deflected from my point. Then you discounted it altogether. Then you started denying it and countering me! Do you even *see* what you are doing?!"

He smiled. A huge smile.

Smiled!

It hit me like a train. *He knows exactly what he is doing.*

He didn't deny it. He was almost proud of himself. He didn't even care that I had caught on, because he was too impressed with himself! He laughed and started talking about a totally different topic (completely unrelated).

Something changed in me that day. My view of our relationship shifted, ever so slightly. I could not live in denial anymore. Devlin had revealed himself in so many ways, but somehow my mind had blocked the reality from sinking in. To acknowledge who he truly was, I couldn't do yet, but my question had been answered.

He knows EXACTLY what he is doing.

Over the next few months our relationship continued to deteriorate in its usual fashion - spiraling out of control with him making some sort of kind gesture to patch things up when it got really bad and he felt me pulling away. I was no longer falling for the same patterns, however. The shift had gotten bigger, and I was starting to see his behavior for what it was, instead of just listening to his words and empty promises. When he would say he was going to do something, I stopped believing him. When he would promise change, it fell on deaf ears. I was not distant towards him, but it was becoming exceptionally clear that he had no intentions on becoming a better spouse, on being more involved with us, or even looking out for our own good. I could not understand his disconnect with us, or why he didn't care about us, because I didn't understand at that time that some people are just pure evil.

26

WHEN THE EMBER GLOWS

There comes a day when you begin to fight back. There comes a day when the little spark within you – the one that had been snuffed out long ago - suddenly flickers to life once again. You don't necessarily know it. It can go unnoticed in the conscious mind for quite some time. You don't feel different. But like a tiny little coal, it silently glows, until one day something comes along and fans it into a flame, and then a raging fire. My day came. It was the day he made a mistake. Although I didn't know it at the time, that day was the beginning of the end - the end of the deception, the end of the façade. And it only took one word.

He called me "lazy." That was all. I mean, yes, it was surrounded by an argument of course, but I don't recall the rest of it. I heard that word, that sentence. And everything changed. He was chewing me out for something I hadn't done – how I had failed to do something he wanted accomplished. I was already expected to drop everything I needed to do, to cater to his impulsive whims. Maybe that day I wasn't able to fit one of his unexpected 3-hour shenanigans into my already packed schedule.

In any case, his end conclusion was that I couldn't get his priorities done in a day because I was "lazy." It was essentially the nail in the coffin.

I had spent my entire life – thirty-some years – believing I wasn't good enough. I was chained to the same self-contempt and shame that had been heaped upon me in childhood. I had learned the lessons of worthlessness my father continually taught me, and I believed I was "broken" and "messed up." But if there was one solitary thing in the world that I knew for sure – it was that I was NOT lazy. In fact, I was one of the hardest-working people I knew. It only took that one accusation to make Devlin's entire house of cards fall, forever.

Something shifted that day, and a great part of it was due to the realization that I was NOT who Devlin said I was. It also dawned on me that nothing I did would ever be good enough for him. And I knew that if I was not useful to him, he would eventually leave. It's funny how our gut knows all these things for much longer than we do. And only when someone takes a rock and shatters the glass bubble we surround ourselves in, do the truths suddenly flood our consciousness all at once.

I had to have a backup plan. I knew that things could not continue forever like they were. Devlin was growing increasingly angry and distant and I never knew when his levy was going to break. I couldn't spend my life continually sick to my stomach with worry about the "what ifs." What if he left and we had no money for rent or food? What if he divorces me and I have to be a single mom? What will happen to my kids? How will we survive?

I couldn't continue to spend endless nights crying and feeling hopeless, and reading books and articles on how to save my marriage anymore. I had done that for years. I had blamed myself. I had tried hard, then tried harder, to make him happy and cater to his every desire. I orbited around his needs and wants. I thought that if I was the "perfect wife" and made his life as happy as humanly possible, that he would choose to love me back and we could have a good relationship. I had spent a decade doing every single thing he asked of me, yet here I was, broken and alone. I had done it all, I had sacrificed everything in me, almost to the point of death, and I couldn't do it anymore. I had to leave off spending my entire life fighting for our marriage, and had to start fighting for my stability – particularly for my children's sake.

This was not a revelation, by any means. There was no sudden moment where I woke up to reality and took my life into my own hands. No lightbulb or "Aha!" moment. I just knew I had hit a brick wall and nothing I had done up to this point had done anything to move our family towards a better future. Our life was like a continual game of Whack-A-Mole and I needed to change the trajectory for the better. I couldn't continue another day of feeling hopeless and lost. So, I gave up the dream of a better marriage, and decided that Devlin was going to do what Devlin was going to do. Fear of abandonment, or his anger, could not continue to dictate every action of my day. "If he leaves, he leaves," I thought. "He's not here anyway but a few days a month. We are *already* living as if he isn't here." It was true, and it was not true. He controlled our life with his anger and domination, but we had missed out on all the good parts that family life should bring– being together as a family, celebrating birthdays and life events, spending time with each other, having support and sympathy and empathy. That part had always been missing. Hoping it was suddenly going to change after ten years, without any interest or effort on his part, was foolish.

My friend had been telling me for the previous two years

that I needed to become financially independent, for my own stability. I guess she could see where things were headed long before I did. Somehow, I embraced the idea that I needed to be able to provide for us, in case Devlin did disappear. And if he didn't, I could still contribute to the family funds so we could get out of debt and not be stressed financially. At that time, Devlin was giving me about $100 to $150 allowance every month or two, for groceries, gas, clothes or other needs for the kids. He controlled the rest of the money and I didn't have access to it unless he asked me to transfer funds from one bank to another, and only for the reason of paying a bill. Bringing in an income would be the first step to relieving my own stress of never knowing about our finances.

Unfortunately, because I had gotten married, then pregnant, at 20, I never finished college. The only job I would be able to find would be a minimum wage one - *not* sustainable with four kids. Devlin also would not let me work outside the home. Somehow, I had to find a way to make money from home, so I could raise our kids and support us.

I spent some time fishing around online, pondering the idea of going back to school. During this time, I discovered a college course for medical transcription at the local community college. It would require a year and a half of college credits, packed into one year. If I took it, I would eventually be able to get a job working from home. It sounded like a feasible solution.

I didn't tell Devlin. I knew he would flip his lid. Instead I spent several months getting all the preliminary requirements met – getting transcripts from past schools sent, filling out paperwork, figuring out financial aid, and jumping through the thousand hoops required to enroll in college. Most of my classes could be done online from home, but there would be orientations and quizzes and tests that I would have to drive to the college to take. I had no idea how I would make any of it work. Devlin forbade me from letting anyone else watch the kids. The college testing rooms did not allow children, of course. Four kids could not come with me to the few classes I knew I needed to show up for. I didn't care. I had to do this. I would figure out the details later.

About 2 weeks before classes started, I told Devlin. Like I figured, he exploded. I had "gone behind his back," I had made a "bad decision," and he could "not allow it." Working outside the home was "against God's plan" and he "couldn't and wouldn't support" me in it. Even after explaining that I could work from home to bring in extra income for the family while still taking care of the kids (I was still hopeful of the possibility our marriage would work itself out), he refused. It wasn't about money or about staying home. It was really about power and control. If I had money, he could not control me the same, and we both knew it. It was the silent argument we both understood, but didn't bring up.

So, he started the threats. He said if I went to class on the appointed day, he would take the kids away. He was vague about what that meant. I said I could leave them with my sister to babysit for 2 hours while I was in class (I only had one!) and everyone would be fine. He refused. He said if I tried to do that, he would show up at her house with the police. I knew he would. But something in me didn't care. His actions were showing on a continual basis that he didn't care about me or our children. Although I had never gone against his wishes, this time I did. My spark was coming back to life. I had made the first decision to get my life back.

It didn't feel that way. It felt like I was rather just stirring up a hornet's nest. I was panicked about what he might do. He was pretty predictable, and things never ended well when he got infuriated. But something inside me pushed me forward. I didn't understand what it was, and I certainly couldn't have verbalized it. But I knew moving forward was the only option. Regardless what fallout came, I needed to go to school. I needed to become financially independent. And I needed to do it *now*.

27

FIGHTING TO BE FREE

I felt devious. I shouldn't have. I had not done anything wrong. But the sense of false guilt from Devlin made my stomach churn. I had taken the children to my sister's house against his will. I needed to go to class and, consequently, had no idea what the day would hold in store. Would he show up at her house in an angry rage, with the police, to take them? Would he bring them back to my apartment or take them back to the moldy shed? No, it wouldn't be an angry rage. He was so good at playing calm and innocent in front of others. He might show up to get the kids, but he would twist the story in front of the cops, and act like he was just a good father trying to remove his kids from a "crazy sister-in-law's house" after his wife "abandoned them." There was no telling what sick scenario he would concoct.

So, when I left my sister's, I hid the kids' car seats. If he did show up to pick them up, the police would not let him drive off without them being in car seats; they were just little. It would at least raise some questions and potentially slow the situation down. This is why I felt devious. I never did things that would intentionally thwart Devlin's will. But I didn't know what else to do. I was not used to having a will of my own. Making a decision to go to a simple college class felt monumental and crazy, and I felt as if I was committing a crime. I didn't understand how the rest of the free world would see it. I felt like I needed to justify such a benign choice.

Ironically, nothing happened that day. Devlin did not show up. This was a bit unnerving and made me suspicious. Devlin always made good on his threats. The fact that he didn't show up made me wonder if he was planning something worse. Silence on his end always meant he was plotting.

The first few weeks of school were a whirlwind of information, input, and trying to figure out what in the world I was doing. By the third week, I finally figured out how things were supposed to flow. By the fifth week, I had a meltdown.

There was *so much* work! I had had *no idea* what full-time college would look like. I had imagined squeezing study and homework in between kids' naps and meal times, and doing a lot of the online work after they went to bed. Wrong. *So* wrong.

The amount of coursework required was huge. I was taking 5 classes per semester and the memorization requirements and sheer volume of material was overwhelming. I was quickly drowning under stress and time pressure. There was no such thing as squeezing homework between activities. Just to keep up, I was having to spend most of the day studying furiously. I spent a lot of time at my sister's house, where the children could run around in the yard and play with their cousins and I could spend a few uninterrupted hours focusing. That is, if I didn't fall asleep. I was *so* tired.

Devlin changed tactics. Instead of fighting me over college, he changed his public storyline. He now acted like he was the martyr, "helping his wife through school." He determined he was going to take the kids to work with him on the days I had to go to campus to take tests, because he was still furious that I would leave them with someone else, even if they were family. A few times he took them to a client's home, with the story of needing to care for them "while his wife was in college," as if he was a good husband working together with me to help accomplish my goals. I didn't fight it, because I didn't know what else to do. He was physically stronger than me and could force them into the car. I wanted to protect my sister and her family from his explosions as much as humanly possible. I still lived in fear constantly of what he would do if I didn't go along with his wishes. It was possible he would leave with the kids and not bring them back. So, when I picked the kids up from his client's home after getting off from school, I smiled and acted like the "good wife," in a "good marriage." I had to get through the year. I just had to.

Desperation is the mother of ingenuity. As the days blurred together, so did my thoughts. Sometimes I would forget a test was due, and I had to scramble to make it to the college on time when I finally remembered. I didn't have time to take the kids to my sister's house, as she lived an hour away. On those days, I had to get creative. I stopped by the grocery store on the way to school and bought gummy bears. My kids never ate candy, so this was a bewildering surprise. Pushing the baby in his stroller, with three other children (ages 6, 8, and 10) trailing behind me, I raced down the hallway of the college and stopped in front of the door of the testing center. Handing each kid a package of gummy bears (minus the baby) I promised them that if they could sit quietly for 15 minutes while mom took her test, they could eat them as soon as I was done.

The door of the room had been left open. I sat down in a chair, ten feet away, and signed onto the computer closest to the door. I could see my kids sitting in the hallway. I could "supervise" them, but they were not technically in the testing room! There is always a way! Although the college staff noted what was going on, I was not breaking any rules, and they said nothing. Amazingly, my children sat quietly leafing through books while I hustled through multiple choice questions about medical terms and meanings, and pharmacology.

That year lasted about 5 years. Well, at least it felt that way. After stumbling through two semesters, I still had to do an internship program over the summer. That was a seeming impossibility because it meant I would have to spend multiple days a week, working 8-hour days, doing transcription for a large company. It meant being away from my kids. It meant a four-hour round-trip drive every day. Devlin would explode. But it was an opportunity for instant employment straight out of school if the company liked me well enough to hire me. I had to somehow manage it.

They were the longest days ever. I got up at 4 a.m., and went to bed at 10:30 p.m. I burned the candle at both ends. Many days I was falling asleep on the road and had to pull over to sleep so as to not cause a wreck. It seemed like I lived at the office and in the car. I snacked while working so I could take naps on my lunch break. So many days I said, "That's it. I cannot do this ONE MORE DAY. I'm done!" with full intentions to not go back. But every day I did.

I talked to myself.

This is how I will get my life back. Don't worry about the next few months. Just go back tomorrow. One day. Just go for one more day. Anybody can do something for one day.

My hard work and exhaustion paid off. I got the job working for a large company. I could support us, alone. The shift to freedom, though unknown to me, had begun.

28

HOLLYWOOD DIDN'T LIE

I felt it, on the day he attacked me. That energy which was different than normal. It walked through the door with him, so tangible it could actually be felt. The atmosphere was thick with an invisible, yet formidable, sense of foreboding. It is difficult to describe, but I knew - *knew!* - something was way off. I wasn't wrong.

He called me that night, not long before he showed up. He said he was in the neighborhood and asked if he could "stop by the apartment and tell the kids goodnight before they went to bed." Because I was trying to avoid any accusations that I was "keeping the kids from him," I reluctantly agreed. I was working from home at my computer, transcribing on second shift. The kids were almost ready for bed. He could stop by for a few minutes, see them, then leave.

When he arrived, I was stuck behind my computer in my bedroom, typing away. He did just as he said - talked to the kids, played with them for a few minutes, and then they went to bed. But he didn't leave. From my bedroom door I could see him fiddling around in the living room. Then he went into the kitchen to make himself a sandwich. A sandwich!

Seriously?!

Something was off. We were barely on speaking terms at this time, and even then, we only communicated about the kids. He had stopped coming up to visit on the weekend for over a month, after another altercation.

I had to wait for my work break before confronting him. In the meantime, he fixed himself food and ate, then fiddled around in the bathroom. I was on high alert. Why was he still here and not leaving? I pulled one earphone off, listening to my dictation with one ear and straining with the other to hear what he was doing.

Many thoughts raced through my mind. Was he trying to bug my house? Set up recording devices in odd places like under the bathroom sink? He was definitely up to something. This was the man who, for years, had boasted stories of how to trap people without getting caught. This was the man whose personal motto was "Leave no evidence." This was the man who never backed down from a fight because he had this unrelenting drive to prove he was right, no matter what the cost. And now he was in my house without a real cause.

He sauntered into my room and plopped down on the floor. I signed off my computer for my break and whirled around in my chair to face him.

"What are you doing?" I demanded.

"I was just eating." He always stated the obvious to avoid answering questions.

"Why are you here? The kids are in bed. You should have left already."

"My van broke down. I can't drive home tonight."

Oh no, we aren't going there. Not a chance.

"What do you mean it broke down?"

"It won't start. It's on the side of the road. I had to walk here."

"Well you aren't staying here." I would not argue against

his story because it didn't matter, he would just start another circular argument that would waste my time for another 30 minutes.

"Look, I'm not going home tonight."

"Um, yes you *are*. You are NOT spending the night here."

He paused for a second, then started his new spiel.

"I have decided it isn't good for me to be away from you and the children. So, I am going to start sleeping here. Even if that means I have to bring a mattress and set it up outside the front door in the hallway, or on the outside balcony. That's how it is going to have to be."

There are no words for this kind of stupidity.

It was a new attempt to shift the power dynamics, or maybe just get a rise out of me, since we were not really speaking otherwise. He wasn't interested in connection or improving our marriage and family, he just felt his control starting to slip away, and he couldn't allow that.

Devlin never entered into a conversation to discuss anything rationally. He just stated how he had decided things were going to be. Then he would throw something absurd in the mix to get an argument going and fuel the fire. The goal was to get me upset and on the defensive. Then he would suggest things so ridiculous that it would throw an element of confusion into the situation. But that was not happening tonight.

"Quit. Just quit. You're not staying. Get your stuff and leave."

"Look, Bella, I don't think that's the way to go about things."

I was getting infuriated because I knew him well enough. I could sit there and argue with him all night but he was *not* going to leave. Which meant I needed to figure out a plan.

I paused.

"Where is your van?"

"It's far away." Vague answers. I felt my anger rising.

"Fine, you know what? When I get off work, I will *drive you* to your van. Or, if need be, I will drive you all the way back to the freaking property if I have to. But let me be clear. You are NOT staying here."

I was getting annoyed with myself because I was showing my irritation. All the while he just kept getting calmer and quieter. A taunting calm. This was the typical way he played the game. He would do things to get me incensed - whether it was trampling over boundaries, being disrespectful, or making up unbelievably ridiculous scenarios. He tried to push all my buttons at once to get me annoyed and simultaneously he would act super calm. Scary calm. The kind of calm that happens in the air before a tornado hits and destroys everything in its path. He would then compare my irritation to his perfectly calculated composure, as a way of "proving" to me how "irrational" I was for being "upset about nothing" - and pointing to his calmness as proof that he must be in the right. It was not a healthy practice of de-escalating a situation - it was a conniving tactic that he used to gain power over me.

It was a stupid game, really. But one that always set me on edge because I knew the calmer he appeared on the outside, the more rage he had built up inside and the more dangerous he became. The slower he talked, the more anxious I got, knowing that his lid was about to blow.

To this day I don't know why I was so bold in responding to him. Normally I just cowered, went quiet, silently stressed or fumed, and became a nervous ball of anxiety. Tonight though, the "something different" in the air had flipped a switch in me. My body was in defense mode and I hadn't even figured out exactly why yet. But energy doesn't lie.

My phone alarm sounded, signaling the end of my break. I returned to my job at the computer. Devlin went into the living room and laid down on the floor. That was where he decided he was going to sleep. He grabbed a pillow from off the chair and stretched himself out across the carpet, as if it was a normal activity to camp out on the living room floor.

It was 10 p.m. I had an hour before I got off work. Only one hour to stress, to think, to brainstorm. Calling the police would not be enough. They might escort him out of the house, but he would have all night to concoct a plan of his own. A plan to vandalize or destroy my car. A plan to go to the courthouse in the early morning hours and try to file an emergency custody order so he would have possession of the kids until a hearing. That would buy him plenty of time to leave the country with them if he already had that in the works. His ultimate weapon of power against me was taking away the kids, and he knew it. And he would definitely try to follow or stalk me to see where I went tomorrow.

No, I would have to wait it out. I would have to find a way to survive until he left the house on his own. Whenever that would be. Hours? Days?

Avoid him. Act as normal as possible. Just survive.

My shift dragged on for what seemed like forever, but finally ended. I shut down the computer and walked into the living room. Devlin was still awake. We began the argument again, him telling me he was not leaving, and me saying he didn't have a choice.

It has always confused me how in broken marriages one spouse will tell the other to "move out" and they actually do just that. Regardless how many times I would tell Devlin to get out, he wouldn't have listened, even though it was MY apartment! It was either physical removal by the police, or he wasn't leaving. He stretched out on the floor, closed his eyes and ignored me.

Some days I wish I could replay this scene, with the strength of the person I am now. Completely different dynamics would exist. But the person I was then, was fearful. Afraid. Dominated. Controlled.

I kept waiting for an answer to pop into my head, but none came. The energy in the air was still strange. Sleep was not an option. If I fell asleep, he would definitely take the kids, without question. He might also bug the house.

I stayed awake. Time stood still. Or maybe it dragged on forever, I don't know. I just remember the last time I looked at the clock it was 4 a.m. Sometime soon after that I passed out from sheer exhaustion.

I was jarred awake by the sound of Devlin's alarm clock at 6:30 a.m. I had gleaned only 2-1/2 hours of uninterrupted sleep. He was stirring. He hit the snooze option on his phone, and it was silenced.

I was in a fog of exhaustion. My eyes burned closed and my head ached from tiredness, but my mind raced. I needed to be awake if he was awake, but my body wouldn't cooperate. I tried to fight off the weariness, but couldn't. He came into the room and knelt down on the floor next to the bed.

Oh God, please. I can't do anything else right now. Please make him just go away.

He wants to "talk." I can't. I am desperately tired. I have to protect my kids. But there is a limit to what a body can tolerate before it forces unconsciousness on you, despite your best efforts to fight it off. He starts talking. I listen, not really hearing, until I pass out.

I felt him before I saw him, his hands grazing me like a snake slithering across the ground. I felt like I would throw up. My body tensed, and I held back the sour wave that washed up into my throat. How did I not know this was his agenda? He was sick. Sicker than sick.

What happened next was what the director of Avalon (the domestic violence shelter), as well as my trauma counselor, labeled "sexual assault." I didn't really know there was such a thing. I knew the term, but didn't know it existed inside of marriage. It wasn't the first time he did such things; I just didn't know it had a name, or that it was a crime. My body had never been my own and that morning was no different.

Oh heck no!

This would *not* be happening today! Somehow, I forced myself into consciousness and found the strength to kick him. Twice.

I jerked myself away, eyes still burning. I felt like I was in a cloud, a fog. Even though the events are etched in my memory, they felt surreal. I remember his phone alarm going off again. He always set multiple alarms because he never heard half of them. He jumped up and ran to the living room to turn it off. I guess he didn't want the kids waking up.

Adrenaline kicked in and forced my tired brain awake. I jumped up too, causing a rush of blood to my head. It felt heavy and pounding. I slammed the bedroom door behind him, and locked it. I was awake, but not alert.

Now what? Now what?

The doorknob rattled.

Now WHAT?

There was silence. Probably only 10 seconds of silence but it felt like much longer. Then the door opened. He had picked the lock.

I remember his eyes. They are burned into my memory because they were hollow. Zombie-like. As if he was possessed by demons. He looked exactly like something off of a horror movie. Except it wasn't something from Hollywood. Those eyes - void of any expression or human-ness at all - really existed. They looked like what a serial killer would have - empty. Soulless. And at that moment, the knowledge of pure evil sliced through my gut and shocked me to my core.

A single sentence streamed through my mind, so clearly it was as if I could actually see the words, in black, bold letters:

I AM GOING TO DIE TODAY.

I screamed, but it was silent. Every siren that ever existed in my mind, went off at the same time, loud and piercing.

I wanted to scream so loud the apartment would shake, but it wouldn't come out. I wanted to instantly attack him with my bare hands and claw him to a pile of flesh on the floor, or grab anything in sight to use as a weapon, whether it be a metal flashlight or a ballpoint pen to stab him with. I wanted to fight with every microscopic cell in my body until there was not the slightest spark of energy or life left in me. But my brain's survival instincts took over instead. Today, survival meant doing something vastly different than fighting back.

I had been trained to survive. And enough training can override any natural impulse, and become the new instinct instead. I was trained for this moment as a 4-year-old child who was raped by her father. I was trained for it as an 8-year-old girl when I was molested repeatedly in dark and perverse ways. I was trained my entire childhood for this. Countless memories of abuse - spanning almost 2 decades - had prepared me for now. My instinct was the do the very thing that had kept me alive so many years.

I froze. I stopped breathing. I became invisible. My heart fluttered to a standstill.

I am not a helpless child this time. I am bigger and smarter than I was then. This won't end here. Not now.

Fight or flight was not an option. Both would end badly. I must engage in the game of "act normal" again, as much as possible, while also keeping him uneasy by giving him unusual responses. I was not even aware I was doing this. It is amazing how our subconscious minds do all the calculating in milliseconds, without our knowledge or consent.

I inched backwards, so slowly I hoped it was not noticeable. My back was towards the wall, but my mind was reaching towards the door.

"What the hell do you want?!"

He was not used to backtalk from me. I was not used to giving it either. He had a weird expression on his face.

"I want to talk."

"I don't want to talk. You need to LEAVE."

He took a few steps towards me.

"Look, things don't have to get ugly," he replied, barely above a whisper.

"Get the hell away from me!"

Freezing somehow did not make me a silent victim. There was something about the atmosphere of pure evil that surrounded him that put me in a different mode. My body knew it. My soul felt it. The words came tumbling out on their own.

He looked at me with an even weirder look. "I just want a hug."

"You're insane. You need to leave!"

Another two steps.

"Give me a hug and then I'll leave."

I'm sure you will, after I'm dead!

I don't say this out loud.

He reached towards me and I jumped out of his way.

"Don't touch me! Get out!" I shriek, decibel levels rising to a whole new pitch.

I was slightly aware of the kids who had woken up and were stirring around in the other room. I tried to judge where they were based on the sounds, drawing a mental picture of what was going on outside the bedroom door. A few were in the kitchen, another was in their shared bedroom. In one fast move I darted towards the partially opened door, and flung myself through it. He followed me into the living room.

"I just want a hug."

"GET THE HELL OUT OF MY HOUSE, *NOW*!"

I was not winning at the "act normal" game because nothing about this was normal.

He paused. I think he realized that the neighbors could hear because he changed demeanor.

He suddenly turned and walked to the kitchen.

What now?

He reappeared in two minutes.

"I need you to give me a ride to my vehicle."

I stared at him in disbelief, realizing again he must be insane.

"No. I'm not giving you a ride anywhere."

"Look, I need to go, but I can't walk all the way there. Just give me a ride to my van."

"No way."

Does he even have a van? Did it break down like he claimed, or is this just a plot too? All I knew was, he was *not* getting me or the kids into a vehicle alone. I wondered if I screamed loud enough if the neighbors would dial 9-1-1. Our daughter appeared in the living room. He turned to her and said "Daddy needs to leave. Do you want to walk down to the mailbox with me?"

No, not happening!

He collected his jacket and bag of stuff he had brought in the night before. He sauntered around the living room, as if stalling. Deciding his next course of action.

I was on edge. What was he doing? What was he planning? Was he actually leaving? This turn of events was strange and extremely disconcerting. He *never* backed down. He was plotting something.

He opened the front door. "Come with daddy to the mailbox." This was part of some game. Devlin never surrendered. I was unaware what his goal was, but I had to stick with my plan.

Act normal as if nothing in the world is wrong.

I nodded to Emma, so she knew to go ahead and walk down with him, but she would not go alone. I followed them out the door and down the stairs, just a step behind. There would be ZERO chance for kidnapping or abduction if that was his next goal.

He slowly walked across the parking lot towards the mailboxes, telling Emma again how his van broke down and now he would have to walk to it, because "Mama doesn't even want to give Daddy a ride to the van." Because after all he was just a poor victim of Mama's hatred.

Whatever!

At the mailbox he paused, and I stood there watching like a hawk, ready to jump at the slightest movement. I called for Emma. She turned around and started skipping towards me. Devlin glanced up at me, still with an odd expression on his face, then turned suddenly and sauntered off behind the dumpster and disappeared. I grabbed Emma's hand and pulled her towards the apartment.

"Move fast!" I hissed. The parking lot had never felt so huge.

We ran past the parked cars and up the brick steps. We reached the apartment door, breathless, and I slammed it shut behind us and bolted the lock. Then I fell apart.

29

ALMOST FREE

I will never know what made him leave that day. I won't know why he chose to walk away instead of beating me senseless and taking the kids. It simply doesn't add up. He had proven over 12 years that he didn't "give up," he never backed down. The only time he changed plans was when he found that doing things a different way gave him a bigger advantage.

Did he see that I wasn't going down without a fight and he wasn't expecting that, and needed to recalibrate? Was he concocting a plan that would be easier for him to "not get caught" in the end? Did he have plans to do things in the legal system to punish and ruin me, but somehow they didn't work out? Not having answers to the puzzle can be frustrating, though I guess in the end it doesn't matter. I was free! Almost.

That day that I officially left him for good and filed for divorce. It was a monumental step towards freedom. But it was only a step. My true bondage was not in physical confinement, or a marriage relationship - it was psychological. Nobody could protect me from the invisible version of him that lived in my head, or his voice that resided there which still told me what to do. It would take another year of battling before I was free from his dominating thoughts.

Just hours after the assault, I went to the women's shelter with one goal in mind - to find resources or recommendations for an attorney. I stumbled through their doors, sleep deprived and on the edge of a nervous breakdown. I told them my situation in a bunch of blundering, and possibly incoherent, words. I wonder now what they thought. Probably my disheveled appearance confirmed my story, I don't know. I was a mess.

They gave a name to my experience: sexual assault. The lady who patiently talked with me clarified that you cannot give consent to sexual relations if you are not conscious. What a concept! I thought sexual assault was what happened to women in dark parking lots, not in a marriage. I had been taught women were "property," awake or asleep. I knew when he violated me in my sleep it felt wrong - and that's because it *was* wrong.

I was afraid he would come after me. I was scared to drive on the road. I looked for his vehicle everywhere, extremely hypervigilant. I had no idea what he would do next; only that it wouldn't be good! I filed for an order of protection and waited for him to be served the papers. I didn't answer his calls. He showed up at my house that Friday and banged on the door, demanding I let him in. I called the police. He disappeared before they showed up.

I knew where he would come next - church. He had not attended there in years, but if he couldn't get to me any other way, he would definitely show up there now, acting as if everything was fine. He knew I usually went to the church meetings every week. My choices were to go to church, or stay home. I didn't feel safe doing either one, but maybe it was safer to be around a lot of people - people who could protect or be witnesses? I definitely didn't want to stay home cowering, sick to my stomach, and expecting him to show up.

I drove to church and went straight to one of the leaders, Jakob. This leader had seen over time the gross neglect and some of the abuses that occurred. He knew Devlin had a fighting spirit and was irrational and impulsive. He had gotten in several arguments with him over the years where Devlin had showed his true colors. I explained the abuse, the fear, and possibilities of what Devlin might do once he was served the papers. I was hoping for encouragement.

"I filed for an order of protection. It is likely he will show up at church this week 'just to see how I'm doing.' I have been told to call the police if he does. They will serve him the order and escort him off the property. We will have a court hearing to determine if they will grant the protection order to be in place for a year, or if it will be dropped."

Jakob snorted. "It's not going to stick! They aren't going to grant you one."

My mouth dropped open as I stared at him. I don't know what kind of response I was expecting, but it definitely wasn't that!

Was my life not worth being granted protection? Did he think I was just exaggerating or making up the abuse? Sadly, over time I found out this is exactly what he thought, but I didn't know it then. I had a gut feeling, though, that I was not really believed.

I was right. Devlin showed up in the middle of church service. I surrounded my four children with "safe people" as a barrier, and went to call the police. It took them fifteen minutes to get there. Meanwhile, Liam, a member of the church, went outside to meet him, and inquired why he was there. He told him that I was concerned for myself and the welfare of my kids, and that it was rather odd for Devlin to coincidentally show up this very week. They had a conversation for several minutes, as Devlin tried to convince him that he had just come to "enjoy worship" with all of us. Eventually Liam came back inside and told me that if I didn't come outside, Devlin would be coming in. He would not try to prevent him. I would not be protected.

What now? What now!?
What kind of man stands aside and doesn't protect?
It was up to me, again.
I can do this this. I can stall.

I felt dizzy and like I was going to vomit, but I needed the police to serve him the order of protection, and that meant acting AS. CALM. AS. POSSIBLE. For another 7 minutes. I could do that. I would find a way. I took a really deep breath, then marched outside. To face the dragon, unarmed.

Devlin had sat down at the picnic table outside the church. I marched over to it, my face like a stone.

"Hi, Bella." He smiled. That innocent, taunting smile.

I glowered.

"Why are you here?" I demanded.

Liam had followed me and sat down on the bench across the table from Devlin.

Devlin started into some typical, ridiculous explanation about how he was just coming to see us, and he wasn't sure why I was upset, and could we talk about it please?

Rage set in. Anger was my way of coping right now. Otherwise I would absolutely fall apart. This was his typical "play innocent" routine and I didn't know if Liam would fall for it or not. But I didn't care. My only goal was to stall.

"What is there to discuss?" I continued. "Did you tell him

what you did? Oh, let me guess, you told him half a story. Why don't you tell him the other half?"

This was the cockiest attitude I had ever displayed towards him. He wasn't sure how to take it. He definitely didn't want to be exposed. He paused, looking back and forth between me and Liam.

"Well," I continued, "did you tell him you showed up at my apartment? Did you tell him why? Did you tell him what you did to me that morning?"

Liam had heard the words "sexual assault" from me earlier, and he knew where this was going. He spoke up.

"Um, I don't need to hear all the details."

"Oh, well I think he should at least be honest if he is going to tell half a story! Why don't you tell Liam exactly what you did?"

Devlin stammered around for a moment, then began his classic circular talking.

Good! He can circular talk to himself until the police show up. Where ARE they??

It is amazing how slowly time can creep by when you need it to hurry. Every second felt agonizing.

Finally, *finally* the police cruiser pulled into the parking lot. I felt my spirit lift. Devlin got a look on his face. A guilty look, then a slight look of fear that he quickly tried to hide.

"Great, someone called the police," he muttered, mostly to himself.

Oh yes, someone did.

The cop confronted him, pulled him aside, and served him the protection papers, explaining the fallout if he chose to be noncompliant. Then he ordered him to leave the premises.

Devlin got in his van and backed out of the parking lot. That's when I lost my composure. I started shaking. I shook so bad that my teeth were chattering, and I couldn't stop. The adrenaline surging through my body suddenly had nowhere to go - it had lost its circuit, and my body had to create movement of some kind to diffuse it. So I shook, uncontrollably, like a leaf in a hurricane.

The police officer came over and talked to me for several minutes about safety and the kids, while I sat there shaking. I just nodded my head. I could barely breathe, barely speak. I wonder if the officer was also killing time, waiting for Devlin to return. I'm sure it is typical for abusers to circle back around after they think the police has already left. Devlin eventually did.

As his van re-entered the parking lot only minutes later, the cop put his hand on his gun, ready to draw it. I was glad for this; I knew the audacity Devlin possessed, and his utter disregard for laws or authority, even though nobody else at that church did.

The cop walked towards the van, ready for a confrontation. Thankfully, Devlin only wanted it noted on his papers that, prior to coming to the church, he had showed up at my apartment and left some cherries and bell peppers by the front door. He didn't want to be charged with contempt for that.

Produce? Seriously?! I was right. I knew he would show up at my apartment, and at church! He is so predictable!

I was usually right about his next move. What I was not right about, was Liam's and Jakob's next move.

30

WHEN YOUR SAFETY NET FAILS

Nothing could have prepared me for what happened next. It came completely by surprise and I had absolutely no mental framework for it. I thought the hardest part of my life was almost over. It was only just beginning.

I had high regard for the church, and I trusted the people in it. They referred to each other as brothers and sisters - as family. Having no relationship with my family of origin (except for my sister who was also a member of the church) I considered them my fill-in family and thought for sure that they would have my back and would protect and support me through this hard time. I never doubted it.

I first felt something was amiss when I told Liam about filing the order of protection, and gave him a heads up that Devlin would probably be showing up at church. I told him I would be signing the divorce papers the following Monday. He cocked his head and looked at me sideways.

"I'm not sure the Bible says anything about divorce for abuse."

I stared at him quizzically, unsure how to respond, unsure

why he even said that. He waited, expecting a response from me. I had a very bad feeling.

"Well... I don't have a Bible verse for you." That's all I could come up with. I walked away. I suddenly knew trouble was brewing.

∼

Sure enough, Liam sent an email to the church board members expressing his alarm at the fact that a member of the church (me) was filing for divorce. The church believed that divorce was only permissible when there was adultery, and even then it wasn't recommended. You were supposed to just forgive and forget. According to them, divorce came about from "hardness of heart," by the "offended party not being forgiving." They also believed you could never remarry, ever, period.

It never occurred to me that my divorce would be going against church beliefs, however. Divorcing for abuse was not even a question in my mind. It was not the "easy way out" - it was the only way out.

Within the following weeks, the church board wanted to talk to me. I panicked. That little niggling feeling in my stomach was rising. There was a familiar feel to it - I was about to get in trouble, though not really sure why - and I felt an emerging sense of dread. I couldn't face it. My body was already capitulating from the stress of the assault, being terrified of Devlin, and panic attacks from PTSD that my therapist diagnosed me with. I was barely holding it together.

To ease my panic, I confronted Jakob in the parking lot after church service. He was on the board and would know what was going on. I needed assurance that this was not going to be as bad as my gut feeling was telling me it would be. I told Jakob I had no problem talking to the board about whatever they wanted to discuss, but that I didn't want Liam there. I couldn't handle having to defend my choice to divorce. Liam didn't even accept the church belief that divorce was allowable for adultery - he believed there should be no divorce under ANY circumstances, ever. I wasn't about to enter into an argument. I didn't have the brain space or emotional fortitude for it.

Jakob looked at me and asked one question.

"Why?"

"Why, what?"

"Why don't you want Liam there?"

"Because I'm not going to try to defend myself against his crazy notions."

This is when Jakob began his own conversation about the sinfulness of divorce. I didn't understand. I tried to sort out his words. I believed he was one of the more intelligent members of the church. Surely… surely he didn't agree with Liam?! I finally interrupted him, not believing what I was hearing.

"What exactly are you saying?"

"I'm saying you don't have a reason to divorce Devlin. At the most, you can file for a separation, but you have to stay married to him. If you divorce him, and he one day decides to marry someone else, you are responsible for making him an adulterer. His sin will be your fault, and you will bear the consequences of his sin. God hates divorce. God will never protect you or your children if you do something that He hates."

God will never protect you or your children.
He can't be serious. This is insane!

"So, you are saying that I cannot divorce because I am going to be responsible for a 'sin' that Devlin *might* commit, *one day?* And that is the reason I have to endanger my life and the life of my kids?!"

I needed clarification.

"The church cannot support you, or help you in any way, if you do something God hates."

I was stunned. Absolutely stunned. I felt my anger rising again. The jealous, protective instinct to guard my children overwhelmed my normally unassertive, timid spirit. The idea of leaving them vulnerable and helpless made me absolutely furious. I was not divorcing Devlin because I had better options to choose from, or just wanted a break from typical marital conflict. Our lives and wellbeing were at stake. This was absolute insanity.

Emotionally locked somewhere between shock, disbelief, and absolute outrage, I spoke the words that would foreshadow my future:

"If I have to choose between the church, or the protection of my children, the church can go to hell!"

I stormed away, and the floodgate of tears opened up. My gut feeling had been right. My world was rapidly falling apart.

At that time, the church was the only social circle that existed in my world. Because we were taught to shun anyone outside the church, I didn't have friends on the outside. If I went against what they wanted, I would be left alone - ALL alone - to face the darkest part of my life with no support at all. It was too much.

So I tried to reconcile. I tried to understand. I eventually agreed to meet with the board and told them what my lawyer advised. I tried desperately to explain myself over and over again, describing in detail what we had suffered and why I needed a divorce in order to protect our family. I sent them documents from other attorneys, explaining the absolute need, trying to somehow convince them to see the necessity. It was a waste of time, but I had everything to lose.

In the meantime, they built a case against me. This is what they always did for people they wanted to get rid of. It is hard to leave a cult. The dynamics are so absurd they don't even make sense; they try to hold on to you, preventing you from leaving, even though they don't want your "contaminating influence" around the rest of their members. They try to convince you of your wrongs, and correct you in front of others - to stabilize their own position and to "cause others to fear" at the same time. Ultimately, they do not want you to leave, because it is one less person for them to control, one less person to finance their endeavors. And one *more* person who goes "out into the world" to warn other people to stay away from them.

Also, there are people within the cult who sympathize with the one being treated cruelly. It is not always easy to convince these people that the leaders are right (though the cult usually succeeds). The cult doesn't want drama; they don't want their time being wasted having to convince people of the evilness of the victim. They want clear black and white boundaries. "Do as we say, and all will be well. Go against us, and you will be sorry."

The smear campaign began. In my gut I knew what was happening, but my mind didn't want to believe it. For a year I stayed in a state of disbelief, with an ever-present sinking feeling in my stomach that made me sick. My stress stayed at a 10 out of 10. I couldn't eat. Sleep was sporadic and fitful. These things together were a combination for a meltdown.

I remember looking in the mirror one day, at my blotchy, tear-stained face, and puffy eyes and asking, "Who the hell are *you*?" I didn't even recognize the person who was looking back at me. I was staring at a total stranger.

It was that day I felt I was hitting a breaking point. There was no escaping my situation, and there was nothing I could do to fix it or alleviate the pain. I had lost my marriage, my hopes, my future, my health, my friends, my entire supportive social circle, and maybe even God. I finally understood why some people do extreme things when they are desperate. There is something about trauma and the way it shatters a person's mind. The anguish feels so unbearable that we try to do something - anything - to distract from it, or numb the pain. Many people turn to alcohol, drugs, or addictions. Sometimes in the thick of our agony and shock, we do things we otherwise never would. And, in those moments, we honestly couldn't care less about consequences.

I glanced at the blades on my dresser. They would work.

My heart fluttered.

Am I crazy?

Sucking in one last, deep breath, I picked them up. Then I began my job.

31

TAKING MY CHANCES WITH HELL

Coco Chanel once said that "A woman who cuts her hair is about to change her life." I think about this now and laugh out loud. It couldn't be more accurate!

I have become more and more amused at how many women I meet, who, during the process of their divorce (or another major life-altering event) chopped their hair off. Not just a trim either, but drastic changes. I don't understand the psychology behind it, but the pattern is undeniable. My guess is that when our world has been turned upside down and is spiraling out of control, our hair may be the only variable we *do* have control over. Unless you are in a cult, that is. Then, you don't have a say in what you want in your life - you simply follow the rules.

The "church" did have rules about hair, but they were mostly unspoken or vaguely defined, so I never thought much about it. Obviously there was a visible pattern of long hair, most without bangs, but there was nothing written in stone that hair had to be a certain number of inches. Just a few comments here and there, or opinions in church services.

When I got the urge to chop my own, I was in too deep of a real crisis to remember their frivolous points. Nor did I think there would be dire consequences over something so trivial. Truth be told though, I didn't care. It has proven to be one of the best decisions I've ever made. It was the revealing issue that broke me free from their power and control and caused me to find out the truth. And it took me one major step closer to freedom.

It felt good to chop it. Something about blades snipping through chunks of hair was satisfying – it had a lovely sound. After I had finished chopping it short, I went to a salon and had them shape it into a typical women's bob haircut. It was shorter than anyone in the church had ever seen it, but it was just a normal cut, nothing extreme. The response however, was extreme. You would have thought I had murdered someone - people wouldn't even look at me at church. Or if they did, they tried very hard to look anywhere but at my hair.

I was quickly called into a church board meeting and subsequently banned from communion, teaching my children's class at church, and from playing the piano during worship services (even though I was the only piano player in the group). I could not attend business meetings where decisions were made: I was no longer "spiritual" enough. Something about short hair screamed "Apostasy!" in their ears and they would make sure I was an example to the rest of the "flock," of what happened to people who were "rebellious."

It didn't stop there. The leaders honed in on both my sister and best friend, convincing them that I had gone off the deep end, and that Satan was deceiving me and would use me to deceive them and others. I was a contaminant to be avoided.

I continued to stay in the same state of shock as before, watching my world and reputation unravel before my eyes, though now it was said I brought my suffering on myself. I guess in a sense I did - I had made a decision for myself for once!

Within the next few months I was visited by a leading minister. We had known each other many years, but he lived out of state and we only saw each other at large church events. Now, however, he called me "out of the blue" to ask to come visit me. I knew where this was going. It was typical apostasy protocol.

When he arrived, his first order of business was to tell me he had heard I was getting a divorce. He had been primed. Jakob had apparently done his job of "informing." I spent the next 30 minutes explaining my entire situation - the abuse, my priority of safety for my children, what my attorney had counseled, the risk of international flight Devlin had threatened, and how we lived in the shed. He listened without speaking. When I finished my spiel, he began his own.

"You do know you can be disfellowshipped because of cutting off your hair, right?"

I stared at him, blankly, as I soaked up what he said. It took several moments.

"What?!"

He repeated himself, and my blank stare turned into a look of disbelief. I was speechless, yet again. Being disfellowshipped meant they believed I would go to hell if I didn't repent. He began citing Bible verses that he believed backed up his position - something about how if a woman has long hair it is a glory and how somehow that was related to God's will. I interrupted him.

"Wait a minute. Not everyone has long hair. You mean to tell me that women in Africa whose hair is way shorter than mine - they don't have glory? Did God forget an entire continent? Are white women more holy - and do they glorify

God more - than black women?" I wasn't about to accept those implications!

He wasn't about to dig a hole for himself either, so he deflected from that point with circular talking. Almost all the leaders of the church used circular talking and arguments. It was their way of confusing people and never answering direct questions. I had learned by now that I would never get an answer to questions that I asked. I could not, however, accept the idea that I would be thrown out of the church over the length of my hair. I needed to get to the bottom line.

"So, you are telling me that the church as whole - besides the local leaders who have their own opinions - isn't clear on whether it is okay for me to divorce someone who has suffocated my children and beaten them black and blue, and abused us in every way, shape, and form, and YET you know that I should be disfellowshipped and will go to hell for *cutting my hair*??"

He blinked. I raised an eyebrow.

"It's part of the rules of the church. When you were baptized and joined the church, you agreed to keep your hair long."

"No, I didn't. There was no question that was asked of me, or statement of faith I made, where I agreed to keep my hair a certain number of inches."

"Oh yes, those are the rules."

Rules. I was done with rules!

I had followed the rules my whole life. The church's rules. Devlin's rules. Everyone's rules. Where had that gotten me?

Within the next few months I was summoned by the board again, to multiple meetings where I was interrogated for hours. They wanted an admission that I knew I was "wrong." They played mind games and word games, projecting guilt onto me in an attempt to make me compliant. It wore me down; I left each meeting crying, confused, and depressed. I advocated for myself in private, speaking one-on-one with members when they were not in a meeting, seeking for them to understand. They would agree with me and say that divorce seemed like my best option, but when they were all in a room together with the church leader, they would take his side, congregating together to bully me into compliance. Their cowardly actions betrayed their fears of becoming the next victim if they outwardly sympathized with me.

To willingly leave the church, or to be cast out meant that you were turning away from God and placing yourself under the control of evil angels and demons. It created huge spiritual implications. Those who had been given "light," they said, and rejected it, were willingly placing themselves in Satan's territory, to be tortured by him, with no protection whatsoever from God. It is utterly destructive to the human psyche, especially to someone with a tender conscience.

I had to get out. My brain could no longer handle the pressure. After church service one day, I scribbled a note of resignation of my membership on a piece of paper and handed it to my friend (who was the secretary of the church). I could not live my life another day being a victim of their constant hatred and revenge. I would take my chances with hell.

32

WHEN YOUR SOUL DEMANDS PEACE

I could not leave without one final meeting with all the members. A church business meeting was called that all members were expected to attend. I wasn't required to show up to the meeting; in fact I could tell by their faces they wished I hadn't. They had grown tired of me by then; I was too much of a problem that they didn't want to deal with. My resignation would be accepted, and I would be shunned by all the people who I had done life with for the past 18 years. But I went for myself. If I was to be shunned from the church from that point forward, I would leave with my dignity intact. I would not walk away without reality being exposed. I was prepared to answer any questions my friends might ask, and defend myself against the false accusations I knew would come from the leaders. I would attempt to save whatever true relationships I possibly had left.

So I went to the meeting where my membership in the church would be cut off. The leader addressed the members, gave his synopsis of the situation, and asked anyone if they had any questions. I was ready to give answers.

No one asked a question. They were silent.

I waited.

More silence.

Nobody cared.

Liam asked to see a show of hands of everyone who agreed to vote me out of the church. Hands raised. My sister. My best friend. Others who claimed to be my friends. I looked each one in the eye as I scanned the room. I wanted to know who stood with me. They didn't care to know why I was being kicked out - many of them had no idea what the "charges" even were – only that the church leader thought I was a contaminant. They didn't care to advocate for me. I was nothing to them. Even after 18 years, I was *nothing* to them.

Finally, *finally* one person (who would later become the next person targeted and disfellowshipped) spoke up, attempting to come to my rescue and defend me. He hoped to generate a discussion, well-knowing that the situation was being skewed. His wife asked to speak as well. The church leader, Jakob, glared, making a mental note of the "sympathizers," then silenced them. He then began his typical circular comments, which were designed to confuse the people in the room so he could bring the discussion back around to his agenda.

One more brave soul timidly spoke up, questioning the way in which things were being handled. This enraged Jakob, who immediately began a new onslaught of lies about me - things completely untrue and ridiculous. If he couldn't convince everyone with distraction and artifice, he would try with outright deception.

"She is in rebellion against church authority! There are things the church board knows that nobody else knows! This is why we have a board - you all trust us to make the right decisions, and she is in a spiritual downward spiral. She just wants to break our church standards. You can look at the sister and tell she has problems! She is unwilling to study anything with us - she says she doesn't have time for that!"

All lies. My anger was rising. I looked around. People were nodding their head in agreement. Surely, I was a lost cause, in open rebellion. Jakob continued his campaign, but I didn't hear it. It was time to leave. There was nothing more to be said. I could not defend myself against outright lies. It would be my word against his, and he had always been much more powerful. Nobody showed an interest in my welfare, whether from brainwashing or cowardice. I was on my own. It was over. I stood up and walked out of the room. Out the door and down the steps, I got in my car, thoughts churning in my head.

I drove away from the church building that day, sad and in shock. My brain could not process what had just happened. How could it be that people I had trusted my whole life could turn against me over an issue they didn't even understand – or even *seek* to understand? I had just lost the only friends I had, and the only world I knew. Yet, a strange and completely unexpected feeling started welling up within me - *relief! I was free!*

33

A MIRACLE CALLED HOPE

There would be more battles. As they say, Freedom is never free. It always costs us something, and always includes a fight, whether it is physical, mental, or spiritual. *But I would win them all.*

There would be the court battle that would literally take years. Devlin fought for custody, for money, and, more than anything else, fought to punish me for breaking free. He had lost control, so he relentlessly sought to control me in the only way he could – prolific family court filings.

There would be a battle for the mind. Devlin's words, as well as the commonly quoted lectures of the cult, repeated themselves in my mind, again and again for years, attempting to keep me bound. My subconscious had been programed by years of lies. It would be no small feat to break away from their indoctrination.

Then there would be a battle for forgiveness - and what does that really even mean? I would not grapple with the commonly cited "forgive and forget" mindset - I already knew that was erroneous and impossible; if nothing else, my post-traumatic stress disorder made sure that forgetting was not an option. You don't just "forget" more than half of your lifetime. However, in order to be free from the destructive variety of anger that kept emerging, I had to learn how to release all of it. Devlin and the church had stolen enough of my life already; I could not allow them to steal my future too.

PTSD was another battle, and one that I despised, as it felt as if my body was betraying me. The truth was, my nervous system had been pushed to its limits, and the panic attacks, muscle weakness, and other symptoms were my body's way of warning me "We can never go back there again - it is not safe!" Knowing this didn't make it any easier, though, when trying to live a normal life, yet having abnormal responses to daily events. There were the nightmares. The triggers. The unexpected sights and smells that made me burst into tears and lose my breath.

There was the battle of grief. I grieved my past, present, and future all at once. I had to come to terms with the fact that my life would never be the same and that there would be permanent losses. I had to accept that my past was a dark hold of fabricated lies and that the future I had envisioned had been shattered. I also grieved the loss of relationships that I had always believed were real, but I found out they were not – the hard way.

Reintegrating back into society was probably the most surreal battle, and more difficult than I ever could have imagined. The confusion was intense and the guilt and questioning of everything I had ever known, felt overwhelming. It would be a long journey back to normalcy.

All these battles - and more - were lined up, to be overcome one by one. But we do not win a battle by looking at the vast landscape and the overwhelming scene to be conquered. Even the most valiant soldier would be overcome with despair that way. Nope. We do it one little step at a time. One decision at a time. That is how we conquer.

For example, we make the choice to show up, to be present - knowing full well the possibility of triggers or pain, but willing to take a chance anyway (when the risk won't cause us more harm of course). We make the choice to say Yes to life, when we can't remember why it even matters. We take a step towards healing, when we are not even sure such a thing exists. And we reach out our hand toward hope, knowing that is what will fuel any of our endeavors.

When I fled the property and shed, knowing the danger I could be facing, I took my first step toward freedom. When I filed for divorce and said, "No more," it was another step. When I questioned the authority of the church, I took another one, and when I made a decision for my own future, it was yet another. It didn't feel like it at the time, but looking back, I can see each one as an act of advancement - evidence that seeds of hope had taken root.

Interestingly, just as abuse can seep in imperceptibly over time, healing is also subtle and gradual. It doesn't appear overnight. Rather the fog slowly, slowly lifts until one day we look around and notice how much clearer things are, and how much better off we are than we used to be. There may be a few instances we can point to in our journey, that we know are major contributing events to our healing, but more often than not we don't feel it. We just live it, day by day, getting stronger - unaware of the miracle taking place.

Experiencing a miracle is to be granted the seeming impossible. They are not always instantaneous. They do not always come in a moment, but like a transforming butterfly, sometimes they are a process that takes time and patience. Sometimes they are seemingly small - little awakenings or sparkles of light - like fireflies, on a dark journey. Sometimes they look like little sparks of faith when we feel we can't go on. Sometimes another name for a "miracle," is *hope*.

34

IN SEARCH OF PEACE

For me, it was simply not enough to get out of violence and abuse. I had to get the abuse - that had penetrated my heart and mind - out of me. It was absolutely crucial to my healing. For so many years my mind had been a battlefield. Trust and hope had been butchered on the altar of evil men's egos, and the pieces of my mind that remained were bloody and broken. I needed to find peace. If real peace was not a tangible reality in this life, then, in my opinion, life was not worth continuing. I had hit my threshold of suffering. If we exist simply to experience suffering and deprivation, enduring decades more of such misery is not rational. Driven to find healing, I often wondered how one finds wholeness after trauma. Was it even an attainable goal, or just a fruitless endeavor?

I heard a story once about two artists who were asked to paint pictures that portrayed "peace." The first painted a scene of a large, still lake, set within the backdrop of tall, majestic mountains. The lake was calm, with barely a ripple; the surroundings serene and tranquil.

The second picture was of a thundering waterfall. The

trees surrounding it appeared to be in constant motion as the gusts of spray from the falls caused their branches to bend and sway. In the corner of the picture, at the end of a small forked twig, sat a calm little bird cradled snuggly in its nest. The first painting, though one could label it peaceful, in reality could simply have been "stagnation." The second painting was one of true peace.

Fifteen years before becoming free, I heard that story, and I had never forgotten it. But now, after many harsh years, this story raised questions for me. Quite frankly, sometimes it also made me angry - mostly because I didn't have answers. How do you actually *have* that kind of peace despite outward circumstances? Is there such a thing as healing from unspeakable atrocities and truly having calmness in your heart and mind? Is peace even a real thing, or just a construct of human minds - an attempt to help offset the brutality of a very dark world?

To those who have *only* known war, the idea of peace is a foreign thing - a strange and curious idea. Yet the fact that our souls crave it in our innermost core, makes me believe it is something that must exist in the universe – something we are wired for. But I also think it something that very few people find. Probably this is why people turn to addictions. They want something to distract from the pain - to find something that will numb their reality. And then, some turn to religion. They lack the joy and peace that they instinctively know *should* exist, but which eludes them. So they seek for peace in 1,000 different ways, ascribing to religious theories, repeating nice clichés and affirmations, promoting good works as a way to palliate the gods or powers that be, or seeking enlightenment by practicing disciplines like meditation and yoga.

I am not one to condemn religion, but it had failed me greatly. In fact, fresh out of abuse, the whole idea of religion was actually revolting to me. Not only did the religion I was taught *not* promote peace, it was actively used to promote abuse and suffering! Some people even excused the exploitation and injuries inflicted over my lifetime, with their favorite cliché of "God works all things together for good to those who love him." Uh, no thanks! That was not a religion I wanted to embrace. How can true peace exist without justice? I could not absorb any more toxic ideas, and the thought of a distant, uncompassionate God sitting on a throne in the stars somewhere, watching the suffering of creation, and calling it a "higher good," was not something I could stomach.

Wading through all the theories, in search for peace and healing though, can be exhausting. Maybe this is why some people give up and embrace the darkness. But I couldn't. I wanted light. I *needed* light.

But how do you find hope and contentment when you cannot deny the intense level of evil that exists in this world? And how do you actually remain serene, in the midst of trauma, despite your outward circumstances? I was done with false religious theories and elusive concepts; I had to find real answers.

Finding real answers begins with asking sincere questions. Could I handle the risk of walking away from everything I knew and believed, trusting that, in the end, genuine peace was a real possibility? What if it meant shattering my entire perspective – could I survive that? Was it even worth it? Was I willing to stand on shaky ground until I could find solid ground? What if the answers I found... were not peace at all, but were darker than the realities I had already survived?

There was only one thing I knew for sure: What I currently believed and practiced, *wasn't working*. And it had never worked. My counselor had always been adept at exposing flawed thought patterns and behaviors, by asking one simple question:

"So... how's that working for you?"

Reality: It wasn't.

It was time to start unraveling the lies.

It was time to become an atheist to the god and belief system I had been taught.

35

BEGINNING TO REDISCOVER SOMETHING I NEVER KNEW

It is only when we become completely unraveled, that we find out what we are made of. What the world is made of. What God is made of. Until then, we fabricate our own beliefs, based on what sounds good to us from our experience. Desperation has a way of deconstructing our mistaken and misguided beliefs, and forcing us to face the cracks in our inadequate theories and beliefs. Ironically, it is also the thing that sets us free.

At some point, our theories and reality have to clash - this is where the "rubber meets the road." Our personal future and existence depend on solid answers. I am thankful for my past desolation. It is what forced me to find real hope. Becoming an atheist to the god I had been taught, set me free. It liberated me from the chains of systemic religion and the accompanying anxiety of peoples' doctrines and assumptions. I was able to let go of my view of a condescending, judgmental, tyrannical type of god that had shaped my mind into believing that misery was honorable. I no longer believe that god exists. I was, ironically, freed to find real faith and spirituality and God…and peace.

As I stumbled through my own questions and dilemmas, I was able to take an unbiased look at the world views that existed, as well as realities that could not be denied. There were things I knew to be true – namely that evil existed. But I was surprised to realize that the counterparts were also true:

Evil exists, but so does beauty.

Darkness exists, but so does light.

Cruelty exists, but so does compassion.

Pain exists, but so does healing.

I could not ignore the horrors of rampant evil that exist in this world. But I could not deny the existence of beauty and wonder either. And when we talk about "healing," nobody talks about embracing the darkness. Surrounding ourselves with evil or cruelty, does not bring wholeness. And if evil religion existed, then surely, too, a life-giving spirituality could exist as well.

My soul craved something genuine and authentic. The polished "faith" and "hope" that false religion had touted for so long, had lost its shine. I wanted the bona-fide gold - a spirituality and a belief system that created love and compassion for humanity – all life for that matter - and birthed peace in my soul, that made life not only survivable, but beautiful. I didn't want to just survive. I wanted a life that radiated hope and healing.

As much as we want to assume that healing is the only way to go, we have to admit that choosing to *not* heal, is a real option also. It is not necessarily a *beneficial* option, but it is a valid one. Choice is ours by birthright. Only when we consciously make the choice to heal, do we become willing to do the hard work that it requires, instead of defaulting to more years of just surviving. I had to choose if I wanted darkness or light, bitterness or peace, despair or hope. Thankfully, I chose hope. My healing journey had begun.

ABOUT THE AUTHOR

Bella Hope Shiloh is an author, speaker, survivor, and advocate against domestic abuse. Between raising her four children, working, and studying to become an attorney, in her spare time she likes to ... What free time? She also enjoys photography and her crazy Doberman, Selah.

....

WEBSITE: BELLAHOPESHILOH.COM
FACEBOOK: BELLAHOPESHILOH_AUTHOR
INSTAGRAM: BELLAHOPESHILOHAUTHOR

Made in the USA
Monee, IL
02 July 2023